GREEN ARCHITECTURE

A GUIDE TO SUSTAINABLE DESIGN

MICHAEL J. CROSBIE

THE AMERICAN INSTITUTE OF ARCHITECTS PRESS

WASHINGTON, D.C.

First published in the United States of America by:
Rockport Publishers, Inc.
146 Granite Street
Rockport, Massachusetts 01966
Telephone: (508) 546-9590
Fax: (508) 546-7141
Telex: 5106019284 ROCKORT PUB

Distributed to the book trade and art trade in the U.S. and Canada by:
AIA Press
1735 New York Avenue NW
Washington, DC 20006
(800) 365-ARCH

Other Distribution by:
Rockport Publishers, Inc.
Rockport, Massachusetts 01966

ISBN 1-55835-127-2

10 9 8 7 6 5 4 3 2 1

Art Director: Laura Herrmann
Design and Layout: KBB Design, Inc.

Printed in Hong Kong

TABLE OF CONTENTS

FOREWORD

Garrett Hardin's famous essay, "The Tragedy of the Commons," shows how a village common pasture suffers from overgrazing because each villager puts as many cattle on it as possible, since the costs of grazing are shared by everyone, but the profits go to the individual. Hardin argues that this is a metaphor for our current global ecology. An impressive body of scientific data on global systems supports Hardin's claim and confirms what native Americans and indigenous people worldwide have known and celebrated for centuries–that we are all interconnected and interdependent.

For the first time in human history we have the technology to monitor and document the problems we are creating in the global commons. For example, we now know that the chlorofluorocarbons we created to increase our comfort by improving insulation and coolants also deplete the protective ozone layer that, ironically, increases the need for energy, insulation, and coolants. It also allows ultraviolet rays to enter our atmosphere, reducing global food production and increasing the incidence of skin cancer and eye disease. In his book *Biologic*, David Wann observed "environmental deterioration is a lack of relevant information . . . [and] poor design is responsible for many, if not most, of our environmental problems." Now that relevant information is becoming available, are we willing to re-examine our designs?

The planet's population of 5.5 billion continues to grow at 1.7 percent annually, doubling our population every 40 years. As this expanding global family consumes resources that exceed the capacity of the commons, architects are beginning to question the design of buildings as sculpture, as objects separate from nature. The debate concerning style becomes irrelevant, if not irresponsible, when our designs create more waste and pollution than the planet can absorb and cleanse. Our grandchildren will care if our designs improve or diminish their quality of life, but will they care if our buildings are postmodern or deconstructivist?

In the summer of 1993 thousands of architects, planners, landscape architects, developers, builders, manufacturers, and suppliers gathered in Chicago on the centennial anniversary of the Columbian Exposition. Some brought their proposals for the future and inspiring examples of projects exploring these new concepts. Many more brought their concerns. There was much discussion about the reliability of new information, appropriate design responses, and much debate about the definition of "sustainable development." The World Congress of the International Union of Architects and the American Institute of Architects adopted a "Declaration of Interdependence for a Sustainable Future" that places environmental and social sustainability at the core of practice and professional responsibility. In addition, the Interprofessional Council on Environmental Design, a coalition of architecture, landscape architecture, and engineering organizations, developed a vision statement to pursue this new ethic "as a multidisciplinary partnership."

The work Mike Crosbie has collected in this book is that of individuals and teams who are seeking to create a new ethic, fueled by the belief that our present designs are destroying the commons. It is significant that Mike has selected the work of North American architects, because it is the "American way of life" that is one of the greatest threats to sustainability. We are setting all the records for consumption, waste, and pollution. Our designs are causing stress, illness, and reduction in productivity, in addition to excessive consumption and pollution. Our community designs are contributing to the isolation, separation, and fear that grips and debilitates our society. Ironically, just as we are becoming aware of the flaws in these existing designs, the developing world is rushing to duplicate the American way of life.

Architects and designers have some very interesting choices to consider at what may become the most powerful moment in human history. Will we choose the traditional role of creating symbols that document the focus of our society? Or will we instead take a leadership role in designing buildings and communities that are worthy of duplication? Will we explore designs that encourage the cultural change required to restore the quality and sustainability of the commons?

As you examine the work of the architects and designers in this book, ask yourself these questions: Are their assumptions about the global environment reasonable? Does their work reflect the new ethic they espouse? Could this direction revitalize the profession? Is this an opportunity for you and the next building you design?

The people whose architecture is represented here do not have all the answers. In fact, most of them have more questions than answers. But they share a common belief that design can create greater efficiency and restore biodiversity. They believe that good design will serve as pedagogy, informing and empowering the users to participate in creating communities that respect and celebrate all life, including the lives of future generations.

— *Robert Berkebile*
Kansas City, Missouri

Mr. Berkebile is a founding member and past chairman of the American Institute of Architects' Committee on the Environment.

EDITOR'S NOTE

The health of any new paradigm in art, science, or politics can be measured by the proportion of spirited commitment to that new world view. The paradigm's vitality can also be gauged by the degree of tolerance for opposing points of view that collect around it. Green architecture, as evidenced by the brief essays in this book, and the work presented herein, has all the hallmarks of a healthy paradigm. The architects and designers most dedicated to this way of practice do not move in lockstep. The debates that they forward here are passionate and compelling, and the work is varied. Occasionally the rhetoric outweighs the accomplishments to date. So it is with all great paradigm shifts.

The object of this collection is to introduce you to a different way of thinking about architecture that takes our role as stewards of the planet Earth to heart, in a way that has never been done in architectural history. True, the architecture of indigenous peoples exhibits some of the same sensitivity to climate and materials. But the form and content of indigenous architecture are not a conscious, deliberative choice on the part of its makers. It is limiting in that it is the only thing its creators know how to make.

We, on the other hand, can select from a plethora of technology and materials. The designers in this book have made a conscious decision to reorder their priorities and make a new path for architecture. Because it is an approach that is sensitive to our planet's capacity to support us, it represents a maturing of the modern mind. As is true of all authentic architecture, it is part of a larger world view that is daily debated in our society.

I want to thank the people at Rockport Publishers and the AIA Press for their help in bringing this collection to fruition. Nancy Solomon, formerly of the AIA's *Environmental Resource Guide*, provided valuable guidance. I am grateful to Robert Berkebile for his illuminating Foreword, and to the architects and designers in this book for graciously allowing their accomplishments — their work and their words — to be included. I am also indebted to the various photographers who generously permitted the publication of their work.

— *Michael J. Crosbie*
Essex, Connecticut

To Forrest Wilson,
who taught me
to keep a stiff upper
heart of oak, which
is a renewable resource.

JERSEY DEVIL

Photo: Kenneth M. Wyner

With my Jersey Devil partners, Jim Adamson and John Ringel, I've been involved in energy-efficient architecture and on-site practice for over 25 years. In architecture school in the 1960s, we followed research in the space program, figuring that a self-contained environment in space would spin off materials and methods for a self-contained environment on this planet. After graduation we started Jersey Devil, a nomadic design/build group making energy-efficient structures, one at a time, and living on site in efficient Airstream trailers and walking to work every day.

When the energy crisis hit in the mid-1970s, we were joined by scores of other Americans who began to innovate in response to skyrocketing fuel costs. President Carter installed solar collectors on the White House and initiated tax credits for energy-saving buildings. With government support, alternative energy enterprises began to spring up and many architects began to consider energy use as an issue in their buildings.

In 1981 Ronald Reagan became president and quickly removed the collectors from the White House, repealed the tax credits, and funneled massive financial support to the nuclear, coal, and oil industries, fostering a bogus energy glut. Architects stopped designing energy-efficient buildings (the media seemed to be tired of them anyway) and postmodernism became the rage (the perfect style for the Gipper, by the way — all face and no space).

In 1988 George Bush took over and the architecture fashion wheel spun around to deconstructivism — an appropriate style for a president who, in a not-so-subtle display of his energy policy, dropped so many bombs on Iraq that it looked like a decon project when he got done.

We had the problems, priorities, and the solutions right in the 1970s. Since that time, the architectural profession has taken so many wrong turns, flirted with so many goofy styles, that sometimes I'm embarrassed to be part of it. (On the other hand, sometimes I think the profession is embarrassed that I am part of it.)

Now Bill Clinton is president and there's a return to energy issues. This time around it's called "green" architecture. It's about time. Buildings consume almost 40 percent of all energy (not including the energy embodied in the materials, shipping, and construction). Nuclear energy, oil, and coal represent death and environmental destruction. Solar energy, recycling, and renewables represent sustenance and survival. If architects want to contribute to the continuation of the species, green architecture needs to be more than a passing style.

— *Steve Badanes*

Photo: Alan Weintraub, funding by the Graham Foundation

HILL HOUSE

TOP: *A low profile blends the house with the topography. The low profile also protects the house from high winds.*

Photo: Alan Weintraub, funding by the Graham Foundation

Sited on a spectacular ridge top, 10 miles from the Pacific Ocean and 50 miles south of San Francisco, this house appears as the hilltop's smile. It is often buffeted by winds of more than 100 miles per hour, so the design cuts the house into the hill to present a low profile to coastal storms. The house sits in a south-facing bowl, allowing the winds to move right over it while allowing generous sunlight.

By following the contours of the ridge and using earth berms, stone from the site, and a sod roof, the house blends into the natural terrain. This strategy reduces heating and cooling loads and provides fire, wind, and earthquake resistance. To compensate for swings in temperature, the house's thermal mass of concrete and stone, and the fact that it is buried into the hill, helps to stabilize its temperature. The larger the mass of the structure, the slower its response to temperature fluctuations.

A Trombe wall that operates primarily by a convective loop is 60 percent below the floor level to allow for direct gain windows above the view. The wall curves from south to southwest and its passive solar components, such as glass and concrete, contrast with the softer, natural forms and materials of the east and north sides composed of earth, boulders, and fieldstone. A wind-powered pump provides water to a storage tank, which is then gravity-fed into the house. Domestic hot water is solar heated.

Section

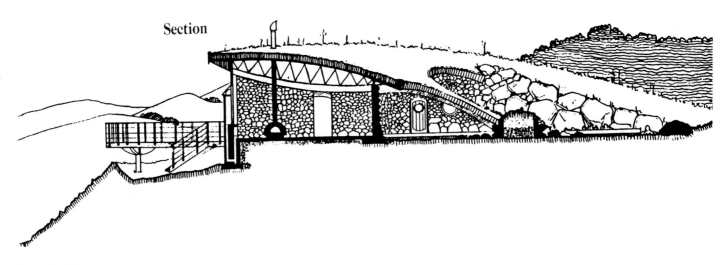

RIGHT: *The inner court is a green oasis. The space is protected from high winds that pass over the house.*
Photo: Alan Weintraub, funding by the Graham Foundation.

BOTTOM: *A view of the court deck from under the "tongue." The hot tub is heated with solar collectors.*
Photo: Alan Weintraub, funding by the Graham Foundation.

LEFT: *The lower portion of the wall is for thermal storage. The wall curves from south to southwest.*
Photo: Alan Weintraub, funding by the Graham Foundation.

BOTTOM: *Banks of windows extend along the hillside elevation. These windows also allow spectacular views of sunsets.*
Photo: Alan Weintraub, funding by the Graham Foundation.

Open trusses give the ceiling its texture. Windows open the house to views along its south side.
Photo: Alan Weintraub funding by the Graham Foundation

1. Entry
2. Living
3. Dining
4. Kitchen
5. Bedroom
6. Study
7. Closet
8. Shower
9. Family
10. Garage
11. Wine Cellar
12. Vegetables
13. Hot Tub
14. Utility

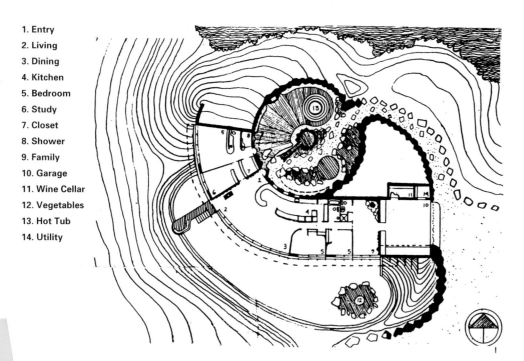

TOP: *Rockwork uses the products of excavation. This material also provides thermal mass.*
Photo: Alan Weintraub, funding by the Graham Foundation

Jersey Devil

TOP: *The house from the air gently protrudes from the hill.*
Photo: Bob Moore

LEFT: *A viewing deck on the hillside offers spectacular views. This element is accessible from the living area.*
Photo: Alan Weintraub, funding by the Graham Foundation

CAMINO CON CORAZON

Baja California Sur, Mexico

TOP: *Handmade saltillo tile for flooring extends throughout the house.*
Photo: Alan Weintraub, funding by the
Graham Foundation

This retirement home is sited on a beach overlooking the Sea of Cortez. The climate of this southern Baja peninsula is hot and dry, with intense sun, fierce winds, infrequent but torrential rains, and occasional hurricanes. The clients wanted an informal house, oriented toward the sea view and breezes, one that would be cooled without air-conditioning.

The house is organized as three sections, one for guests, another for living and entertaining, and a third for the master bedroom. The three sections are separated from each other by breezeways. Each section can be opened to an oceanside terrace and to the breezeways by means of folding mahogany and glass doors, turning the entire house into a covered porch.

Construction of the house is concrete frame with block infill. The truss roof is covered with a tiled concrete slab. These materials provide a thermal mass that helps keep the house cool in the hot weather and warm in the evening when the mass radiates heat back. The roof, the house's most distinctive feature, is a system of lenticular trusses covered with a reinforced concrete slab. The underside truss chords are lath and cement plaster, forming a double roof that is ventilated by natural circulation. Air enters through the grilles at the roof ends and exits through vents in the parapets and through the chimney form at the house's center. This eliminates solar heat gain through the roof, keeping the house cool without insulation.

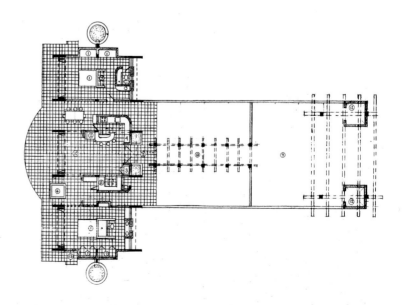

The view from one end of the house to the other demonstrates the building's openness. A tile floor absorbs warmth from the sun during the day, reflecting it back at night.
Photo: Alan Weintraub, funding by the Graham Foundation

LEFT: *Detail of the tile roof, with venting in center and at edges. This roof's structure is composed of lenticular trusses, which give it its unique shape.*
Photo: Alan Weintraub, funding by the Graham Foundation.

BOTTOM: *View from the study. Open windows funnel prevailing breezes throughout the house.*
Photo: Alan Weintraub, funding by the Graham Foundation.

TOP: *View from the dining room toward the Sea of Cortez. The house can be easily converted to an open pavilion.*
Photo: Alan Weintraub, funding by the Graham Foundation.

LEFT: *View of the complex with its butterfly roof. Roof water is directed to a cistern below the scupper.*
Photo: Alan Weintraub, funding by the Graham Foundation.

LEFT: *Cortez sea view with bifolding doors closed. Breezeways zone the house into three separate wings, all with views.*
Photo: Alan Weintraub, funding by the Graham Foundation.

BOTTOM: *View from the study. Open windows funnel prevailing winds throughout the house.*
Photo: Alan Weintraub, funding by the Graham Foundation.

TOP: *Northeast elevation. Screens in the front provide privacy and natural ventilation. The entry is through a courtyard planted with natural vegetation.*

Photo: Alan Weintraub, funding by the Graham Foundation.

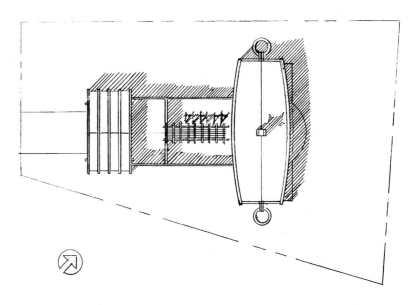

PALMETTO HOUSE

Miami, Florida

TOP: *Overhangs shade protected areas for outdoor living.*
Photo: Alan Weintraub, funding by the Graham Foundation.

RIGHT: *An awning protects the woodshop from heat gain. Native plants grow close to the house for privacy and shade.*
Photo: Alan Weintraub, funding by the Graham Foundation.

This house for a writer and a woodworker is on a two-acre site dense with palmettos, pines, and pepper trees. The clients wanted a house that recalled the traditional "cracker" style tin sheds of Florida, with climate-responsive features. The first floor is devoted to utility spaces and a woodshop, while the second floor contains living spaces and a studio loft.

Keeping the house cool and comfortable in this hot and humid climate is achieved through the use of a radiant barrier that restricts the transfer of infrared radiation across an air space by reflecting it, rather than absorbing and re-radiating the energy into the interior — a quality known as "low emissivity." Most building materials, such as glass, wood, and paint, have high emissivity and radiate energy easily, making them ineffective as radiant barriers. This house employs foil radiant barriers in the roof construction and most of the walls. This makes the best use of radiant-barrier technology because it is exposed to the most solar radiation. In order to purge heat buildup between the foil and the roofing, a balanced combination of continuous soffit and ridge vents was used.

Screened porches on the east and west sides act as thermal buffers, and are kept open to the house for most of the year. To encourage cross ventilation, awning windows with anodized aluminum frames and gray fiber screens are used opposite each other. Twelve paddle fans increase air movement on still days. Hot water is provided by solar collectors.

A pink spiral stair leads to
the loft. Natural light floods
the loft and illuminates the
floor below.

Photo: Alan Weintraub, funding
by the Graham Foundation.

LEFT: *The end of the roof over-hang contains custom lighting. Its metal cadding reflects heat in this tropical climate.*

Photo: Alan Weintraub, funding by the Graham Foundation.

BELOW: *View of roof's gable end with venting for heat exhaust.*

Photo: Alan Weintraub, funding by the Graham Foundation.

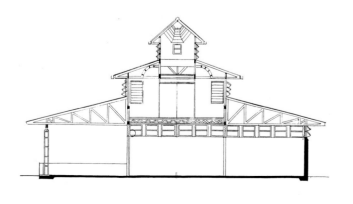

The loft's perforated floor allows hot air to vent through louvers. The floor grill also permits light transmission to the floor below.
Photo: Bill Sanders

TOP LEFT: The kitchen uses domestic renewable hardwoods for cabinetry and flooring. Paddle fans help air circulation.

Photo: Bill Sanders

TOP RIGHT: View from entry porch out to the stair landing.

Photo: Alan Weintraub, funding by the Graham Foundation

LEFT: View from kitchen/living areas to entry porch.

Photo: Alan Weintraub, funding by the Graham Foundation

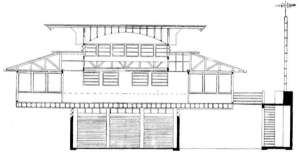

TOP: *The loft is suspended by trusses and accessed by a spiral stair. Since there are no full-height partitions, views, natural light, and breezes enter the building freely.*
Photo: Bill Sanders

LEFT: *Screen porches on the east and west act as thermal buffers. This space also provides sitting areas protected from insects.*
Photo: Bill Sanders

HOUSE IN THE KEYS

TOP: *The entry canopy is made of wood and sheet metal, with tiles made by the client. The galvanized steel structure can be seen above.*
Photo: Bill Sanders

This new beachfront home/studio for a couple of potters incorporates a concrete shelter that was built by the Red Cross after a 1935 hurricane. The older building contains new living, kitchen, dining, and study spaces. A new structure incorporates a ground-level pottery studio, while above are private living spaces with incredible views of the ocean.

The second level awning windows encourage ventilation. Ceiling fans, closets louvered on both sides, and interior partitions that do not extend to the height of the vaulted ceiling, all increase air flow. Generous roof overhangs, soffit and ridge vents, and a radiant roof barrier above the insulation plane of the vaulted ceiling, keep the upstairs cool even during hot, muggy summer months. This allows the house to stay comfortable without air conditioning.

A galvanized screen structure extends across the second story on the house's bay side, wraps around the corner, and continues across a covered bridge to a stair tower. It appears again on the carport bridge rail. This "Living Screen" is an armature for tropical vines that provide shade, privacy, oxygen, and a buffer against highway noise and car exhaust.

Other sustainable features of this house include a recycled plastic deck on the original Red Cross house, solar-heated water, and thermal mass construction of reinforced concrete, which not only aids in cooling but is also hurricane resistant. A recycled 1971 Airstream trailer hoisted onto the old carport roof and bolted through it serves as a self-contained, energy-efficient guest quarters. Taxis Architects of Miami were the associate architects on this project.

This stair tower connects the studio wing with the original Red Cross structure. The screen is an armature for tropical plants.
Photo: Bill Sanders

NATCHEZ STREET PAVILION

Seaside, Florida

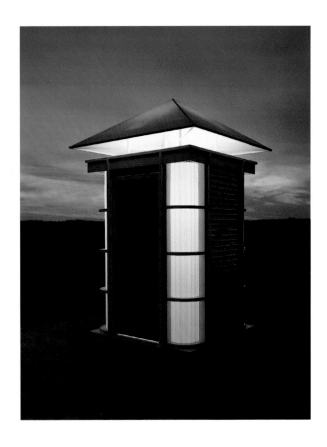

This 185-foot walkover allows for public beach access while protecting the vegetation, such as dune grasses and sea oats, that is critical to holding the dune in place. The decking and seats are made of juniper (eastern white cedar), harvested from fallen trees in the swamps near Apalachicola, less than 100 miles from the site, and locally milled and dried. Juniper is naturally rot resistant and nontoxic in contrast to the pressure-treated wood that is normally used for waterfront decking. Pressure-treated wood is considered hazardous waste — landfills won't accept it and burning it is not allowed. In addition to its low embodied energy, the juniper retains its "pet shop" smell as beachgoers abrade it with their sandy feet.

The parasol structure was fabricated in state from recycled aluminum. The marine alloy structure is lighter, stronger, and more durable than the more typical wood pavilions of Seaside. The light skeletal frame can withstand winds in excess of 140 miles per hour. The aircraft paint should be maintenance-free for 20 years — an incredible feat in this highly corrosive environment. The woodwork is assembled with stainless steel nails and screws.

At one end of the walkover is a restroom and changing room. The site is one of several on the Gulf of Mexico where sea turtles lay their eggs. Lighting on the pavilion is controlled by a photocell and is limited to 40 watts so that newly hatched turtles will head seaward where they're supposed to, rather than towards the lights of the pavilion.

TOP: *The bathroom illuminated from within at night, controled by photocells.*
Photo: Bill Sanders

LEFT: *Detail of seats of rot-resistant and nontoxic juniper. The parasol is made of recycled aluminum.*
Photo: Bill Sanders

HOAGIE HOUSE

Suburban Washington, D.C.

This residential complex, composed of a main house, gate house, and guest house, is located on a six-acre wooded and hilly site. The long main house edges out over a rock outcropping on a concrete corbel and is connected to its sibling buildings through tubular bridges. All of the buildings are clad in natural cedar siding.

The house's organizing element is the Roto-Lid, a computer-operated shading skylight invented by Jim Adamson that automatically moves with the time of day and the seasons. The Roto-Lid is based on an equilateral triangle with a rotating panel of insulation that has three positions. Always on an east-west axis, during a winter day the panel faces north, admitting the sun's warmth. On winter nights the panel rotates to seal the triangular chamber from the interior, preventing heat loss. On a summer day the panel faces south, admitting northern light and minimizing heat gain. The anodized aluminum panels, which have three inches of insulation, are counterweighted and in perfect balance so that very little power is needed to rotate them.

Like the Roto-Lid, the house is linear and has long north and south exposures. Inside, the Roto-Lid enlivens the house with generous sunlight. Other "green" features of this house include a drip irrigation system for extensive interior landscaping that contributes to healthy indoor air quality; water-source heat pumps for heating and cooling; earth berms on the house's north side to naturally insulate it from cold winter winds; and slate flooring over concrete for thermal mass for collecting the sun's warmth during the day and radiating it back at night.

TOP: *The house's central spine, with the Roto-Lid in position. The glassy spine naturally illuminates the interior.*
Photo: Kenneth M. Wyner

BOTTOM: *The Roto-Lid distinguishes the house's rooftop spine. South exposure has an in-ground pool near family room.*
Photo: Kenneth M. Wyner

The house's west end corbels up from its concrete base. This end of the house overlooks the wooded site and offers a view of the sunsets.
Photo: Kenneth M. Wyner

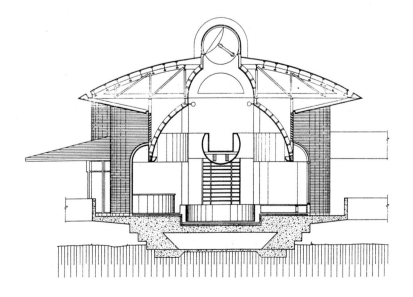

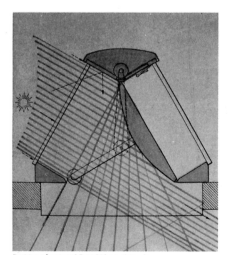

Position of patented Roto-Lid on winter day.
Drawing by Jim Adamson and Greg Torchio.

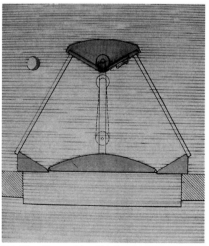

Roto-Lid position on winter night. *Drawing
by Jim Adamson and Greg Torchio.*

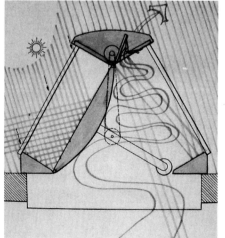

Roto-Lid position on summer day. *Drawing
by Jim Adamson and Greg Torchio.*

RIGHT: *Natural stone work is used in house's central fireplace.*
Photo: Kenneth M. Wyner

BOTTOM: *The house's east end, showing the garages and rear entry. Cedar is used as natural cladding on the exterior.*
Photo: Kenneth M. Wyner

OPPOSITE: *The main house stretches out along the site, with the guest house at the left. The south elevation is the most private side of the house.*
Photo: Kenneth M. Wyner

WILLIAM McDONOUGH ARCHITECTS

New York, New York

Design leads to the manifestation of human intention and, if what we make with our hands is to be sacred and honor the earth that gives us life, then the things we make must not only rise from the ground but return to it as well — soil to soil, water to water. Everything that is received from the earth can be freely given back without causing harm to any living system. This is ecology. This is good design.

Vitruvius described the art, wisdom, and practice of building with mass to anticipate the scope and direction of the sun. The ancients knew how thick a wall needed to be to transfer the heat of the day into the winter night, and how thick it had to be to transfer the coolness into the interior in the summer. Bedouin tents are astonishingly elegant and provide light, shade, air movement, shelter from rain, and are transportable; five things at once with simple, renewable materials. Even the Gothic cathedrals can be seen as experiments integrating great light into massive membrane.

One challenge has always been how to combine light with mass and air. This experiment has displayed itself powerfully in modern architecture, which arrived with the advent of inexpensive glass. However, at the same time the large sheet of glass showed up, the era of cheap energy was ushered in too. Because of this, architects no longer depend upon the sophisticated use of the sun for heat or illumination.

Fortunately, we can use nature itself as our model and mentor to redefine our design principles, and, in doing so, can find that there are three defining characteristics in "natural" design from which we can learn. The first is that everything we have to work with is already here — the stones, the clay, the wood, the water, the air. All materials given to us by nature are constantly being returned to the earth without waste.

The second characteristic is energy, which allows nature to continually cycle itself through life. This energy comes from outside the system in the form of perpetual solar income. Nature does not mine or extract energy from the past, it does not use its capital reserves, and it does not borrow from the future.

Finally, the characteristic that sustains this complex and efficient system of metabolism and creation is "biodiversity." What prevents living systems from running down and veering into chaos is a miraculously intricate and symbiotic relationship between millions of organisms, no two of which are alike.

As designers we should ask ourselves how to apply these three characteristics of living systems. Only by searching for answers can we come to terms with our rightful place in the natural world.

— *William McDonough*

WAL-MART "ECO-MART" RETAIL STORE

Lawrence, Kansas

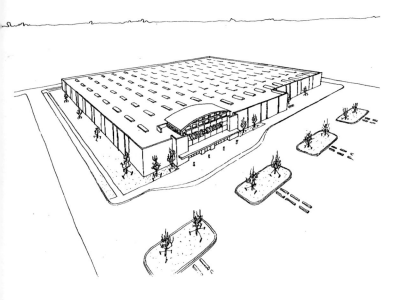

TOP: *Perspective view of current Wal-Mart "Eco-Mart" store. Skylights are used to diminish the building's demand for artificial light.*

OPPOSITE BOTTOM: *View of renovated store as future housing. Open courtyards and heavy landscaping create shared, communal spaces.*

William McDonough Architects was retained as design and environmental consultant to BSW Architects of Tulsa, Oklahoma to develop a prototype, environmentally conscious retail store for Wal-Mart. The new store addresses a number of programmatic and building construction issues that set it apart from most buildings of this type.

Among the store's features is a wood roof structure in which all of the forestry products used — including glu-lam beams, I-trusses, sawn lumber, and plywood — are from certified sustainably harvested forests. In converting the standard Wal-Mart store from steel construction, which uses 300,000 BTUs per square foot, to wood construction, which uses 40,000 BTUs, thousands of gallons of oil were saved just in the fabrication of the building.

Newly designed skylights provide substantial daylighting for over 50 percent of the store and are connected to a photosensitive dimming system for the fluorescent lighting. As the sun streams in, the fluorescents are shut down when not needed. An ultraefficient HVAC system uses no chlorofluoro-carbons (CFCs), which have detrimental effects on the earth's ozone layer.

The "Eco-Mart," as it has been dubbed, also contains a small recycling center that sorts and bales 15 different types of materials, including much of the packaging used for the items sold in the store. In addition, the building is designed to be converted into housing or other purposes if its use changes at any time in the future.

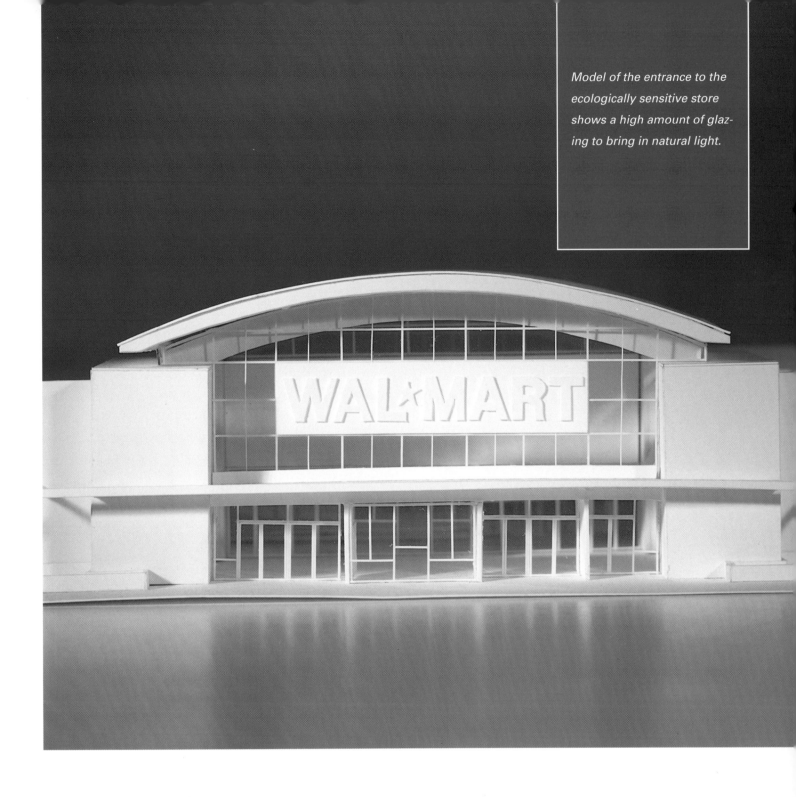

Model of the entrance to the ecologically sensitive store shows a high amount of glazing to bring in natural light.

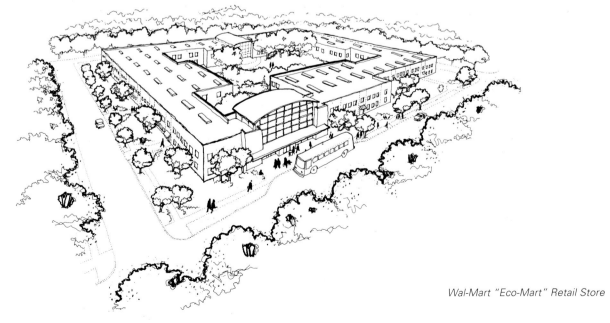

FRANKFURT DAYCARE CENTER

T his Frankfurt daycare center is unique in that it is designed to be operated by the children. It contains a greenhouse roof that has multiple functions: it illuminates, heats both air and water, cools, ventilates, and shelters from the rain, just like a Bedouin tent.

Recognizing the importance for children to look out the windows in the morning to see what the sun is doing that day and interact with it, the architects enlisted the help of teachers. The teachers told the designers that the most important thing was to find something for the children to do to interact with the building. The children have ten minutes of activity in the morning and ten minutes of activity when they leave the building, opening and closing the system, and both the children and teachers love the idea.

Because of the solar hot-water collectors, the architects asked that a public laundry be added to the program so that parents could wash clothes while waiting for their children to get out of school. Because of advances in glazing, it was possible to create a daycare center that requires no fossil fuels for operating the heating or cooling. Fifty years from now, when fossil fuels will be scarce, there will be hot water for the community and a social center. And the building will have paid back the energy borrowed for its construction.

OPPOSITE: *The hall of the daycare center is its main reception space. The skylights have hinged insulation panels that swing into place.*

TOP: *A section through one of the daycare wings shows some of its environmental design features. The stone wall at the center collects heat during the day to radiate it back at night.*

CENTER: *Isometric of the complex's three wings. This north side shows how roofs are open to northern light, which provides even illumination to classrooms.*

BOTTOM: *Site plan of the complex reveals the wintergarden which is found below the glazing on the building's north side. The center element contains solar collection units.*

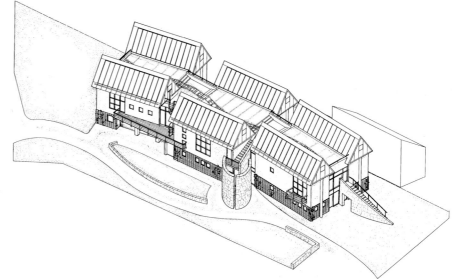

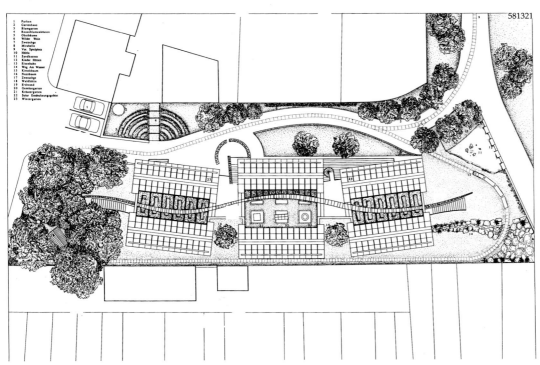

OBIE BOWMAN

I am sure that most of the values I bring to my work are outgrowths of my own experiences, and many reach back to the fondest memories of youth. I grew up in California's San Fernando Valley at a time when agriculture was the predominant sense of the landscape and the Los Angeles River was a wonderful source of life and boyhood experience. Early on I became fascinated by nature, especially fish, reptiles, and amphibians. As the years went by I was aware that many changes were occurring, but was unprepared to predict the consequences. Upon my return from college it was clear that I had actually been witness to the complete replacement of the agrarian landscape with desolate suburbanization. The old river was now a concrete flood channel where people dumped old shopping carts. The trauma of this realization created a personal paradox with which I have struggled ever since: a desire to build and a need to preserve the natural landscape.

Almost everywhere, our buildings have no message or meaning. They inevitably ignore the nature of the place. We don't design and build organically, but often repeat what someone else has done somewhere else. Instead of using our brains to improve our lot, we continue to mindlessly destroy the uniqueness and specialness of the landscape by building expanses of faceless suburbias. This leads to our loss of place in the landscape.

Lawns and foundation plantings are almost always alien substitutes for the natural landscape, and, consequently, all too often require supplemental water, insecticides, and fertilizers. The poisons and fertilizers build up toxicity levels in the local water systems while irrigation water is piped down from someplace farther north or east where it is ostensibly not needed. I know we all grew up with this kind of landscaping from childhood and that it is now part of the American way; but just like racial prejudice and cigarette smoking, it doesn't necessarily have to be that way in the future.

We have an ethic for our dealings with one another but not with our dealings with the natural world. At this point we desperately need a morality concerning man's relationship to the land and the plants and animals that grow upon it. And how our architecture responds to it. It is not our divine destiny to plunder the earth.

— Obie Bowman

Photo: Charles Callister, courtesy of
the California Redwood Association

SPRING LAKE PARK VISITORS' CENTER

Santa Rosa, California

TOP: *Amphitheater extends beneath overhang of southeast-facing solar collector. The collector provides daytime heat for the building.*

Spring Lake Park is a 320-acre flood control facility owned by the Sonoma County Water Agency and operated by the Sonoma County Regional Parks Department. The idea to build a visitors' center in the park was over 20 years old when the project finally gained momentum in 1988 with the formation of a citizens advisory committee. They asked for a place that facilitates learning about nature and exemplifies a sympathetic relationship to the environment.

The project is located on the northwest slope of an ancient lava flow, now wooded with oaks and buckeyes, overlooking Spring Lake. The forest's character is maintained by placing the building away from existing parking and restrooms and allowing only pedestrian access. A welcoming circle of boulders is located just up the access path. Closer to the building is a grottolike storyteller's cavern where rangers can introduce visitors to the facility before they enter the building. The center opens on to a small amphitheater from which paths lead to a view deck overlooking the lake.

The visitors' center is an instrument for teaching the processes of nature. The building harmonizes with its setting by placing its solid walls into the natural grade and using sloped glazing to retain the translucency of the woodland from outside while allowing views up into the surrounding boughs from inside. Exterior redwood shading fins screen the sun and sky glare and become finer and less translucent with height, simulating the scale change of the surrounding oaks and buckeyes. Centrally located is a tentlike fabric structure housing a research/exhibit preparation area. Natural materials and natural aging processes are used throughout. Trees removed from the site are used to form an overhead canopy for the storyteller's cavern.

Because heating is required only during visiting hours, room air is heated with a southeast facing solar collector. An earth cooling tube and thermo-siphoning system provides cooling and ventilation, and shaded glazing allows for nearly 100 percent natural daylighting. Backup heat is provided by a wood-burning stove with fuel recycled from the site.

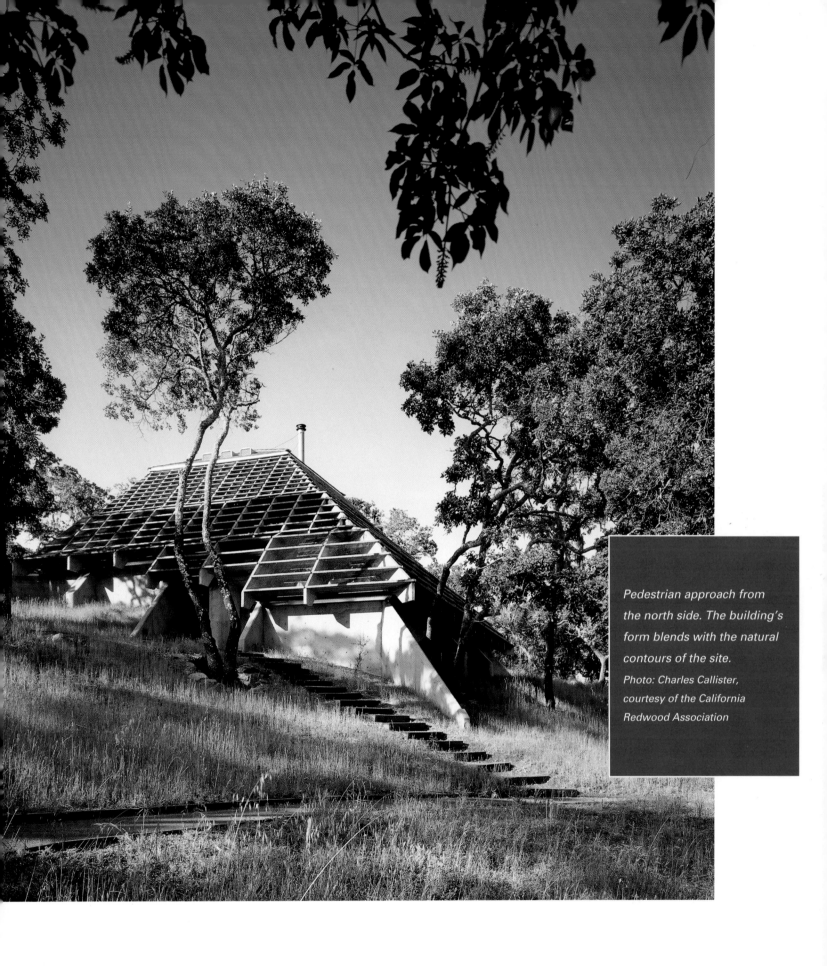

Pedestrian approach from the north side. The building's form blends with the natural contours of the site.
Photo: Charles Callister, courtesy of the California Redwood Association

TOP: *Center as it steps down the hill-side from the south. Plantings around the building are native grasses.*
Photo: Charles Callister, courtesy of the California Redwood Association

LEFT: *The visitors' center amid its wooded context. The center offers views of Spring Lake.*
Photo: Charles Callister, courtesy of the California Redwood Association

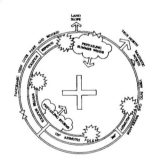

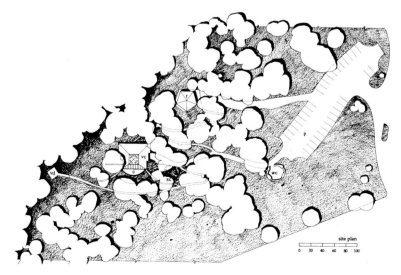

SPRING LAKE PARK VISITORS CENTER

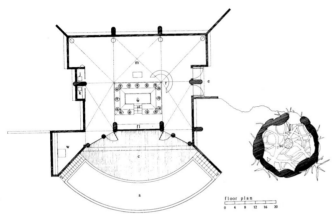

SONOMA COUNTY WATER AGENCY

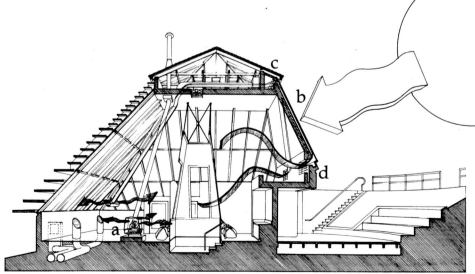

heating section

a: Woodburning Stove with Catalytic Combuster
b: Solar Air Heating Collector
c: Supply Manifold with Blowers
d: Intake Manifold with Filtered Openings

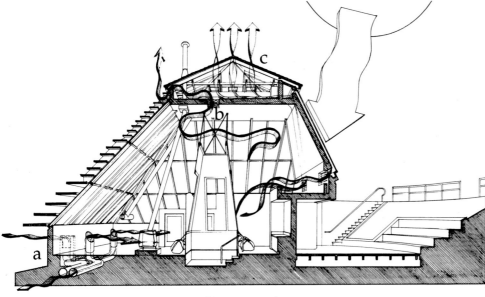

cooling section

a: Intake via Underground
Cooling Tubes

b: Ceiling Fan discharges Hot
Air through Eave Vents

c: Automatic Louvers vent Collector
via Roof Vents

CASE BEDROOM/BATH REMODEL

Kentfield, Marin County, California

An existing 1950s residence sits on an acre of land and, over the decades, has become sequestered in a mixture of native and introduced flora. The owners asked for a remodel/addition that would enhance the exchange with their surroundings and maximize enjoyment of the daily bathing and bedding ritual.

The existing bathroom was removed to enlarge the bedroom and a 430-square-foot extension was added to accommodate the new bathroom. The floor steps down allowing the addition to occur at ground level, under an extension of the existing roof line.

The dominant feature is a central fireplace, which is composed around the four Aristotelian elements fire, air, earth, and water. These elements are envisioned as the material embodiment of the sensual qualities hot, cold, dry, and wet.

A see-through fireplace links bedroom and bath. Large, vaulted skylights contrast with the low ceilings and afford upward views into extensive pine boughs above. Native boulders from a local quarry give definition to the shower and spa while also linking inside and out.

TOP: *Shower celebrates the four Aristotelian elements-fire, air, earth, and water. Dual shower heads drop directly down from the skylight.*

LEFT: *Bathroom is lighted by an arched skylight that provides views up into pine boughs above.*

BOTTOM: *View from bedroom continues through fireplace and shower to garden beyond.*

BRUNSELL RESIDENCE

TOP: *Interior columns are from an old stand of dying eucalyptus trees.*

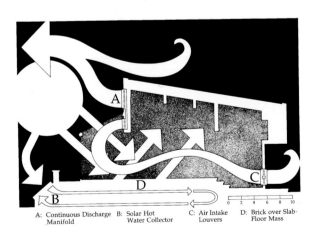

A: Continuous Discharge   B: Solar Hot   C: Air Intake   D: Brick over Slab·
    Manifold   Water Collector   Louvers   Floor Mass

The overall landscape consists of narrow meadows between the coastal hills and ocean bluffs interrupted by periodic cypress hedgerows. Cold northerly winds blow throughout the spring and summer. The corner lot lies on the ocean edge of an extensive rural subdivison.

This 2,800-square-foot weekend/retirement house was designed and built for two gourmets who have no children of their own but typically have entire families as house guests. Accordingly, separate guest room and master bedroom wings were required, each connecting to a large common area.

The heart of the common area is an oversized kitchen island (intended to reduce separation of spaces and people) that always acts as a vital part, if not the focus, of common area activities. Cooks and noncooks alike readily interact around the perimeter of the island, whether they be at the dining, bar, or living areas. Natural materials and natural aging processes are predominant: columns were obtained from a stand of dead eucalyptus trees, and fireplace brick chunks came from a grog pile.

This house is a partial expression of the architect's personal search for a desperately needed ethic between our expanding populace and ever-diminishing natural environment. Besides minimizing loss of the native flora and fauna, it strives for visual harmony with the sweep of the coastal hills and responds to the specific conditions of its site.

The building form, influenced by setback requirements, creates a wind foil that deflects wind up and away from the southerly decks. The meadow displaced by the building footprint has been replaced in the form of an earth-covered roof. Only indigenous plants have been used. The house effectively uses solar space and water heating, natural ventilation, and natural lighting, with a radiant floor backup system. Excess roof water percolates back into the ground as does much of the water falling on the gravel driveway and parking court.

Westerly facade of the house looking down the south coast line. The building form creates a wind foil to deflect winds away from the decks.

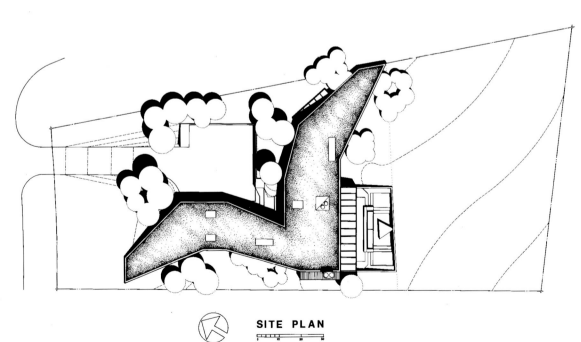

SITE PLAN

RIGHT AND BELOW: *Made of recycled brick meltdowns retrieved from a grog pile, fireplace is expressive of owners' personalities.*

BOTTOM: *Clusters of intake air louvers at sides of entry doors help house to cool itself naturally.*

RIGHT: *Sloped glazing of study allows interior space to project beyond the main perimeter wall of the house.*

BOTTOM: *Kitchen is designed to minimize separation of cooks and guests This common area joins guest and owner's wings.*

LOUIS RESIDENCE

Sea Ranch, California

An 1,850-square-foot passive solar vacation house with solarium, island kitchen, and interior spa was designed for a middle-aged couple with grown children. The site is on the edge of a young Douglas fir forest and an open sloping meadow. A patch of ocean is visible to the southwest from the highest part of the property.

A triangular solarium is oriented toward the ocean view while the two wings of the house extend from this focus at 90-degree angles. These two roof forms sympathize with the sloping land while three thermal chimneys echo the rising tree line. The chimneys cool the solarium by bleeding off heat, thereby allowing the solarium to be contiguous with the other interior spaces. Blowers at the chimney intake grilles can alternately cycle hot air through rock heat storage beds beneath the floor. Roof-mounted solar panels provide hot water, and backup space heating is provided by a wood-burning stove.

The materials include concrete slab with wood-framed walls and exposed timber roof. Exterior materials are cedar siding, cedar shingles, and sod over the living area, which merges with a contained berm of site-excavated soil. Interior materials include Mexican pavers, vertical grain Douglas fir flooring, gypsum board, and exposed Douglas fir roof decking.

TOP: *View of ventilation chimneys used to bleed off unwanted heat from the solarium. The roof forms echo the sloping site.*

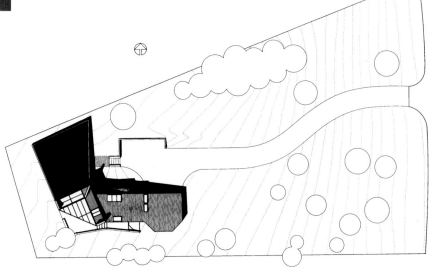

Solarium/dining room is contiguous with adjacent rooms. This space offers a sweeping view of the ocean.

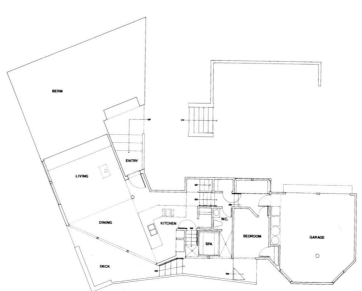

Louis Residence   59

LEFT: *View from across the meadow from the west in the spring.*

BELOW: *The sod roof of the living room harmonizes with the meadow. The chimneys echo the rising tree line.*

Most rooms have sky-lights for natural lighting and tap into the thermo-siphoning ventilation system.

KISS CATHCART ANDERS ARCHITECTS

Photo: Richard Barnes

The words ecology and economy derive from the Greek *oikos*, for house, and both words refer to the relationship between the house or household and their external environments, whether natural or societal. The two words are functionally linked as well: in the long run, architecture that is ecological must be economical. Buildings that are energy-efficient or resource-efficient at the expense of simplicity and cost will not be meaningful solutions to environmental problems.

In our work, we try to find solutions to specific problems that also apply to general issues. Tight budgets and restrictive programs have forced us to balance new technologies with existing methods and materials, and the demands of new methods with traditional design priorities. We try to express new materials, technologies, and energy management paradigms in our architecture, but not at the expense of function or comfort.

Since 1984 we have been involved in the integration of photovoltaic (PV) technology into architecture. PVs, which produce electricity from sunlight, are active devices that are complementary to other solar and energy-efficient technologies. Unlike most other energy-related technologies, however, PVs have architectural implications. They can be used as building materials, adding value by performing more than one function. While capturing sunlight, they can also shade windows, capture heat, or diffuse daylight. PVs have the potential to change the energy paradigm of contemporary buildings from one that minimizes and mitigates the effects of the sun to one that turns outward, gathering as much solar radiation as possible. For the first time, buildings can shift from consuming to producing energy.

The art of environmental design lies in the balanced application of the many available techniques and technologies. Super-insulation, daylighting, solar thermal devices, advanced mechanical systems, and PVs are a palette of strategies to be applied according to climate, energy demand, local energy costs, and, most importantly, to the program and architectural idea. It is important to be realistic in assessing the value of each: solar thermal devices can be energy-efficient but difficult to operate and maintain. There are tradeoffs between cost, toxicity, embodied energy, and durability in many building materials. PVs are relatively expensive in areas with cheap electricity and low insolation. But a realistic assessment also includes intangible values. In the real world, economy is not restricted to money: better health, productivity, security, and public image are real and valuable benefits. From this perspective, economy is critical to a building's ecology, and an ecologically sound building is inherently economical.

— *Gregory Kiss*

Photo: Richard Barnes

PHOTOVOLTAIC MANUFACTURING FACILITY

TOP: *View toward front door, with entry stair on the right. Curved stainless steel wall separates reception from factory floor.*

Photo: Richard Barnes

The Advanced Photovoltaic Systems (APS) Manufacturing Facility is an unprecedented project housing the largest thin-film photovoltaic (PV) production line in the world. The PV panels produced within will be used in applications ranging from consumer and building products to utility-scale power generation fields. The building, a 70,000-square-foot concrete and stainless steel structure, is the first phase of a project that will incorporate a connected Training and Technology Center in the future.

The production line is a flow line process, utilizing advanced robotics to produce two million square feet of PVs each year. The modules are 2′ 7″ x 5′ 1″, making them the largest monolithic PV modules produced in this country. The size of the modules makes them useful for large-scale applications of all kinds, including integration into buildings.

The building is designed to serve as a prototype for emerging PV building technology. Central to the sustainable design features of the building is a cubical control facility sheathed in a PV glass curtain wall and interpenetrating the tilt-up concrete volume of the production facility. PV skylights in the cube roof and a PV entry canopy combine with the curtain wall to produce sufficient power for lighting and air conditioning, rendering the cube an energy-independent "building within a building." The majority of PV wall panels are installed within an insulated, double-wall curtain wall system, allowing for convective ventilation of thermal buildup behind the panels. A section of PV modules in the curtain wall plus those modules in the skylight are installed without the second insulating layer. These panels demonstrate the PV module's ability to serve as translucent glazing, transmitting a pleasant, diffused natural light to the cube's interior.

TOP: *Near the entrance, the PV awning with the PV-clad cube rising above it.*
Photo: Richard Barnes

RIGHT: *Sunset view of the factory, showing the service side of the building. The building's long lines orient elevations to solar exposure.*
Photo: Richard Barnes

TOP: *View of PV awning from above. Paving pattern shows sunpath diagram and a schematic depiction of the PV's row of silicon atoms.*
Photo: Richard Barnes

LEFT: *Floor of a PV cube, showing diffused light admitted through PV glazing. PVs can thus be used for shading.*
Photo: Richard Barnes

BOTTOM: *West end view of the PV awning, with PV panels to the left and stainless steel canopy to the right.*
Photo: Richard Barnes

RIGHT: *Underside of PV awning from entry. PV technology has the added value of adapting well to architectural elements.*

Photo: Richard Barnes

BOTTOM: *Service bar on the building's north side, with loading docks and doors to mechanical and materials storage space.*

Photo: Richard Barnes

CONFERENCE/CULTURAL CENTER AND HOTEL

Northern Caifornia

TOP: *View looking north of the exhibit hall. Underside of PV sawtooth roof, which also provides daylighting.*

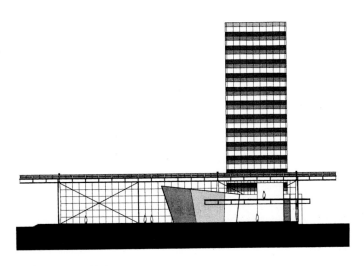

This building complex combines exhibition space and meeting facilities with a theater and a hotel. Located on the downtown waterfront of a U.S. west coast city, it links an existing ferry terminal and a waterfront park to the city hall and government center.

The hotel is a thin slab with maximum east and west exposures for its vertical curtain walls. The curtain walls combine opaque and semitransparent PVs with clear glass in a flush-glazed system, internally ventilated from floor to floor by convection dampers at the head and sill of each window. Hot air from the wall cavity is directed in or out, according to demand.

The conference center is a glass shed with a prominent overhanging roof glazed with PVs and clerestory windows. The roof system provides daylight to the interior while shading the perimeter walls, which are glazed in a graduated dark-to-light glass for shading and privacy. The sawtooth roof is supported by box trusses tilted to support the PVs while providing drainage sufficient to keep the modules clean.

A spine connects the two buildings to the ferry terminal and serves as roof to the hotel lobby, as shelter to the hotel and conference drop-off area, as a mezzanine structure in the conference center, and as a parking and walkway canopy to the terminal. It demonstrates the flexible ability of PVs to be extended beyond a building into the site.

Large-area, thin-film PVs are used throughout. Uniform appearance, large size, and low cost are the principal advantages of this type of PV. Modules are assembled into ten-foot-square glazing units for roof and canopy applications and into 3' x 5' units for wall applications. The PV power produced is equal to peak summer demand. The complex pays only for relatively small amounts of off-peak power.

RIGHT: *Aerial view from the south with PV parking structure in foreground and hotel in background.*

BOTTOM: *Twelve-story hotel slab facing east-west for PV curtain wall, which is ventilated for exhausting heat.*

DESIGN HARMONY

Photo: Michael W. Cox

For us, environmentally conscious design is a passion. Our approach is holistic, balancing health, ecology, and spirit in architectural design. Directing the firm's energies toward environmental projects was a conscious decision; in fact, it was the basis of our partnership. This focus has required us to evaluate each potential project with respect to how it aligns with our own values of achieving more ecological responsibility. It has sometimes meant turning down commissions from clients who did not share an interest in environmental concerns.

Every project is approached with respect to five critical issues: siting, energy efficiency, indoor air quality, alternative building materials, and waste reduction. In addition, we feel strongly that "team building" is paramount to each project's success. This belief has led us to create unique partnerships in almost every project, often with people possessing widely varied interests and expertise. This "partnering" leads to the best use of each team member's time and talents, usually yielding the most innovative results. Humor is an essential component of our work style. We believe that every job has opportunities for fun — both for us, and for our clients. This concept is carefully nurtured; humor is necessary in order to maximize every project's outcome.

With a strong commitment to the education of laypersons as well as future architects, we have taught architecture at North Carolina State University School of Design and Duke University and have lectured and consulted nationwide on architecture and its environmental impact. Our goal is to educate the profession and the public about ecologically viable architecture — the design and construction of a built environment that is not only healthy for the inhabitants but for the earth as well.

— *Cheryl Walker and Gail Lindsey*

THE BODY SHOP, U.S. HEADQUARTERS

Wake Forest, North Carolina

TOP: *Office interior with daylighting monitor. Ample use of natural light cuts the building's energy consumption.*
Photo: Doug Van de Zande

ABOVE: *Interior warehouse area painted with high reflectance non-VOC paint.*
Photo: Doug Van de Zande

OPPOSITE BOTTOM: *Interior front entry with recycled tile flooring. Low work station partitions allow clear sightlines throughout the interior.*
Photo: Doug Van de Zande

Beginning with the concept of utilizing "embodied energy," The Body Shop selected an existing 125,000-square-foot office/warehouse for renovation into a new national headquarters and manufacturing facility. An environmentally conscious company that produces naturally based cosmetics and skin care products, The Body Shop was a client dedicated to manifesting its environmental principles in both the production of its products and the construction of its building.

To realize the challenges of an environmentally sound, economical, and fast-track renovation, Design Harmony partnered with Clearscapes Architecture (architect of record) and Clancy and Theys Construction (contractor). Design Harmony's role was to generate design ideas, and to provide a comprehensive framework in which all team members (owners, architects and designers, and contractors) could evaluate their decisions environmentally.

"Daylighting monitors," oriented north to south for the full length of the building, maximized daylight as the primary lighting source for the building's offices. The exposed roof structure was painted with high-reflectance, nontoxic paint to maximize artificial and natural light dispersion. Low workstation partitions in open office maximize daylighting.

Metal halide indirect lighting, with daylighting photo cell controls, was used in the office area, supplemented by high efficiency task lighting. Occupancy sensors in offices, conference and training rooms, and labs turn lights off when the rooms are unoccupied.

Replacing existing waterclosets with new, low flush waterclosets conserves water. Many interior materials and finishes are nontoxic salvaged and recycled-content, including no VOC paint in the warehouse, carpet from recycled plastic pop bottles, and lobby tile made from recycled glass bulbs.

*Renovated exterior and
front entry of 1970s building
"recycled" into headquarters.
Photo: Doug Van de Zande*

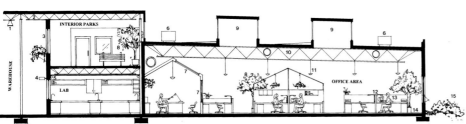

LEGEND

1 - Reused existing high efficiency HPS
   lights in warehouse, with group re-
   lamping program

2 - Exposed structure with high
   reflectance, non-toxic paint
   maximizes light quality

3 - New openings in interior and exterior
   walls admit more light into
   mezzanine and warehouse

4 - Energy efficient LED Exit Lights

5 - Occupancy sensors in offices,
   conference, training and labs turn
   lights off when unoccupied

6 - Reused existing roof top units with
   added economizer units increase
   efficiency

7 - Enclosed offices with clerestories and
   interior windows admit maximum
   daylight

8 - Plants function as natural air filters

9 - New daylighting monitors full length
   of building maximize natural light
   in office area

10 - Full height exposed ceilings with high
   reflectance paint maximizes
   natural and artificial light in work
   areas

11 - Indirect, metal halide pendant fixtures

12 - High efficiency task lights at work
   stations

13 - Reused workstations from previous
   facility, low partitions maximize
   light dispersion

14 - Carpet from recycled PET plastics

15 - Parking remote from building to
   improve air quality at operable
   windows

THE BODY SHOP, RETAIL STORE

Cary, North Carolina

TOP: *Recycled floor tile is used in the store's interior. The choice of paint for the interior contains no or low volatile organic compounds.*
Photo: Michael W. Cox

For the design of a Body Shop retail store, owners Jan Davidoff and Julie Merricks (former environmental attorneys) asked Design Harmony to examine the feasibility of modifying "store standards" to incorporate more environmentally sensitive building materials. This was felt to be more consistent with the company's established social and environmental initiatives. Specific considerations were nontoxic finishes, sustainable wood sources for millwork, recycled-content materials, energy-efficient lighting, and water conserving fixtures.

Regionally available recycled composition marble tiles (in green and white) replaced the standard Italian marble floors. Tile was installed with a nontoxic grout. Natural linoleum flooring replaced vinyl composition tile (a petroleum derived product) in the storeroom and the bathroom. Pine shelving finished with a water-based sealer was also used in the storeroom in lieu of particleboard shelving containing formaldehyde. Nontoxic adhesives and caulks, and no- and low-VOC paints were used throughout the store.

New mechanical ductwork insulation was wrapped on the exterior (rather than the standard interior) of the duct to prevent growth and dispersion of molds and mildew through the HVAC system. Low-flush toilets and low-flow faucets were specified to conserve water.

This store integrated a handful of "green" materials and strategies, and these were found to be cost effective, functional, and aesthetically pleasing. This spurred The Body Shop U.S. Headquarters to look at a national "environmental audit" of their retail stores, and to consider development of a new environmental "prototype" store.

RIGHT: *Front entry, in its mall environment. The store is a showcase for environmentally sensitive interior design.*
Photo: Michael W. Cox

BOTTOM: *All display counters and shelves are made of woods from renewable sources.*
Photo: Michael W. Cox

DOUGLAS POLLARD ARCHITECTS

Toronto, Canada

Inherent in the concept of "green" architecture, or in the categorization of "green" architects, is the implication that there exists a distinct category of approach to design, outside the main body of architectural thought, that can be separated, identified, and catalogued. Perhaps it is that all designs that isolate such consideration as respect for the site and for the balance of nature and the beauty of the planet from other consideration of human needs may be shortsighted and inadequate. I believe that it should be the architectural norm, rather than the exception, that limiting abuse to the site, the users, and the planet is simply a part of design philosophies that simultaneously explore appropriate forms, materials, and spatial interplay to create uplifting architecture.

Ideally, environmental considerations currently labeled "green thought" should be the basics for every project. We should seek solutions that minimize energy consumption and maximize the performance of building components and systems. We should pursue architecture that utilizes materials that create minimal damage at source, and during manufacture and transport, as well as maximum enjoyment at their point of destination.

As with so much human activity, there is considerable waste in architecture. Great amounts of energy are devoted to dead-end stylistic journeys and meaningless sculptural essays. If this wasted energy was treated as a resource and was redirected into the consideration of primary human and planetary needs, there might exist the possibility, if not the probability, of cogenerating great architectural works that truly address the issues of energy, waste, and a healthy future.

As a species, we started out having to yield to nature's forces. Little by little, we developed methodologies to tame aspects of nature to serve our needs. Along the way many lessons of cooperation, balance, and respect were learned. Too many of these lessons have been ignored as our own "inventiveness" led us down a number of dangerous detours. Reminders of these lessons are now all around us: disappearing forests, dying lakes, ozone depletion, dwindling resources, sick buildings. It is time for a review and a retracing and reintegration of basic principles into the design process.

Architecture that cooperates with and embraces nature can lift the human spirit to a higher plane than that which is based on temporary stylistic and wasteful fads. It is of no small benefit that it can simultaneously and significantly contribute to the arrest of the terminal consumption and destruction of the planet.

— *Douglas Pollard*

Photo: Jeff Goldberg/Esto

BOYNE RIVER ECOLOGY CENTRE

TOP: *Wood and steel mesh trellis support vines to shade the triple-glazed windows during summer.*
Photo: Jeff Goldberg/Esto

Historical building forms, radically improved with advanced technologies, are at the core of this design. Housing classroom space for up to 200 students who visit there weekly for lessons on the environment, the building serves as a powerful example of appropriate stewardship. Creating all of its own power from wind and sun; water-heating, cooling, and ventilating itself by natural methods; and processing its own waste with an in-house bioregenerative, machineless system, this building conveys vividly the message that near-zero impact architecture is not only feasible but immensely delightful.

Its 16-sided plan, reminiscent of numerous early building forms, efficiently encloses 6,000 square feet. A centralized circulating and gathering space allows the entire perimeter full access to the daily swing of the sunlight and breezes, with views in all directions. At the center is found the spiritual hearth, which also supplies supplemental heat when required.

The sod roof, supporting a glazed cupola, directs natural convective air movement as well as even light distribution. An occasional assist from four 10-watt fans for ventilation is all that is needed in the coldest months. The building envelope uses airtight building technologies, high insulation, and high performance windows. This efficient skin, combined with the building's high mass and earth coupling, eliminates the need for mechanical heating and cooling systems.

Reliance on daylight, in combination with energy-saving fixtures, electronic controls, and the absence of machinery lowers electrical demand to the point where it can be totally served by a small wind machine, a 14-panel photovoltaic system, and a microhydro generator supplying a battery storage facility.

Hot water demand is supplied by solar panels and radiators around the fire working in turn according to the season. Waste is treated by a living machine comprised of tanks, clear cylinders, an indoor marsh, and a pond in the building's greenhouse. This biological environment removes and decomposes various contaminants, providing water of the same purity as that which enters the building initially.

RIGHT: *A view from across the pond. The building is visible through trees during spring but is hidden during summer.*
Photo: Jeff Goldberg/Esto

BOTTOM: *View from above. The building's sod roof blends it into the hillside and foliage.*
Photo: Jeff Goldberg/Esto

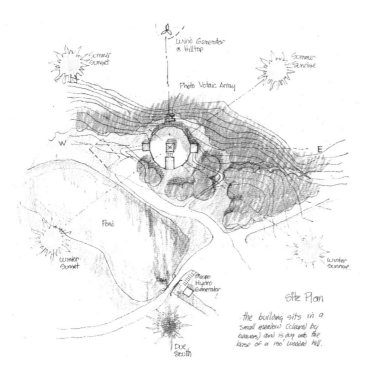

the building sits in a small meadow (cleared by beavers) and is dug into the base of a 150' wooded hill.

TOP: *Bioregenerative waste treatment equipment, visible from classrooms, central space, and exterior provides valuable lessons in waste management and nature's food cycle.*
Photo: Jeff Goldberg/Esto

RIGHT: *Teaching space, with sink that looks out onto waste treatment room. The floor is patterned with icons of rocks, fire, and sky.*
Photo: Jeff Goldberg/Esto

Central space is the focal point of the building, distinguished by a fireplace.
Photo: Jeff Goldberg/Esto

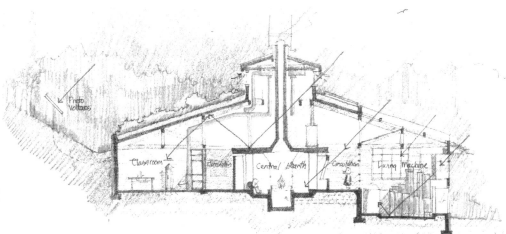

North to South Section
The building dug into the hill is coupled with the earth for warmth, covered with earth + foliage for cooling + exposed to the sun for heat, light + spiritual renewal.

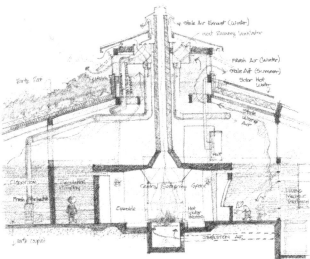

Section Through Central Hearth
Space is created for casual overlooking, evening recovery sessions.
The cupola, hearth + chimney provide heating, cooling + ventilation + daylight.

TRAVIS PRICE ARCHITECTS

Takoma Park, Maryland

Photo: Bruce Katz

While the "greening" of architecture has made remarkable strides over the past 30 years, technological breakthroughs are not a part of the forefront, and for good reason. The techniques and technologies of saving energy and using renewable resources efficiently have become so simple that we no longer need to worry about cost-effectiveness or technological success. The engineering lifeboats have been invented and reinvented to the point of measuring BTUs on the head of a pin. Indeed, we have never paid less per BTU in our history and yet more people are embracing green architecture than ever before. If technology and cost competitiveness are not the pressing breakthroughs for green architecture, then what is?

One growing innovation over the past decade is the subtle integration of renewable energy resources with poetic metaphor. Making green architecture synonymous with gracious architecture continues to be my major design intention. It is hoped that my work produces a poetic design statement through the synthesis of diverse, energy-efficient techniques and indigenous metaphors.

Historical construction methods, such as south porches and building on piles, will not only amplify energy savings when exaggerated but will produce an aesthetic that has an environmental dialogue with the past, as well. South-facing windows–a traditional convention of cold climate buildings–when exaggerated will create a passive-solar structure. My architecture blends these historical environmental strategies with images and metaphor evoked from the client.

Working with nature continues to be the inspiration as well as the solution. Harmony with nature is achieved by being harmless to the environment both in the use of renewable materials and by constructing buildings that operate on little, if any, fossil fuels. More importantly, these energy-conscious strategies work best when they become inseparable from the poetry of the architecture. This is green and gracious architecture, nature alive and dancing in today's complex built environment.

— *Travis Price*

PRICE RESIDENCE

Takoma Park, Maryland

This 3,400-square-foot home was built in Takoma Park's historic district. The neighborhood is eclectically composed of Victorian, Art Deco, and bungalow/Greco homes, as well as 1950s brick ramblers. The design intention was to be as "jazzy" as possible within the existing neighborhood imagery to the furthest extent that the stringent historic district commission would allow. This was further disciplined by the tight 22' x 45' footprint allowed on the narrow lot.

On the exterior, the rustication of the building base, steep roof slopes, and classical columns complement the local historic buildings. A simple suburban temple with dynamic symmetry faces the street front and expands open on the south facade with a continuous highwaylike deck that bounces sunshine into every room.

The interior is an explosion of the solar box through the mixture of color and form changes. A New York loft-feeling is evoked in the open floor plan and in the use of Bauhaus-inspired fixtures and materials. Natural light is bounced throughout the house.

The house is unique in the neighborhood because it integrates renewable energy strategies for both heating and cooling with the local context. The heating strategies employed include super-insulation with six inches of batt insulation, an acrylic stucco and foam insulation skin, Low-E glazing, and a tight geometric configuration. The house gets passive solar heating through the south-facing wall of windows. This gain is retained by motorized insulation curtains (R-11). Cooling strategies include the use of high ceilings and ceiling fans, operable windows for cross ventilation, and south overhangs for shading the summer sun.

A house within a house within a house, a metamorphosis from historic neighborhood to minimalist home with walls bathed in light, the Price residence is now included on the official Historic Takoma tour.

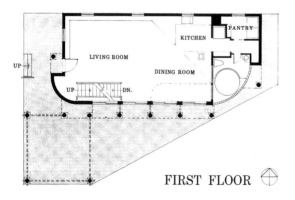

FIRST FLOOR

OPPOSITE TOP: *The entry facade alludes to the architecture of the neighborhood. The width of the house is only 22 feet.*
Photo: Ping Amranand

TOP: *The south side of the house is glazed for passive solar gain. A continuous deck extends across the back.*
Photo: Ping Amranand

RIGHT: *The interior of the first floor is light-filled. The openness is meant to evoke the atmosphere of a New York loft.*
Photo: Ping Amranand

BERMAN/GENTNER ADDITION

The house is located in a densely populated neighborhood where eclectic architectural styles have continued to evolve with numerous additions and renovations. Lot lines are tight, allowing little room for sculptural additions and so instead demand a decorated shed approach. The functional requirements for the addition were an enlarged eating area with family area on the first floor, in combination with a substantial new master bedroom and bathroom upstairs, and a spiral stair to a new deck at grade outside.

The design strategy for the addition was to mix the neighborhood's architectural eclecticism with fragments of the existing home exposed within the addition. An abundance of winter sunlight was an imperative as well. The dining area retained its brick construction–partially enclosed in strips of white maple and mahogany. While formal dynamic symmetry is arranged with the glazing, humor and humanity are maintained by color and chaos. The spiral stair and sunken piano-shaped deck allow for an easy transition to the captured garden below.

Passive solar heating, super-insulation, and a wood stove, and operable windows and fans, maintain thermal comfort along with low energy consumption. The addition boasts the world's smallest greenhouse (1' x 14') with a full utilization of every square foot of ground the zoning ordinance would allow.

TOP: *First floor dining area. Maple and mahogany strips cover brick structure.*
Photo: Ping Amranand

RIGHT: *Interior view of dressing temple at master bedroom.*
Photo: Ping Amranand

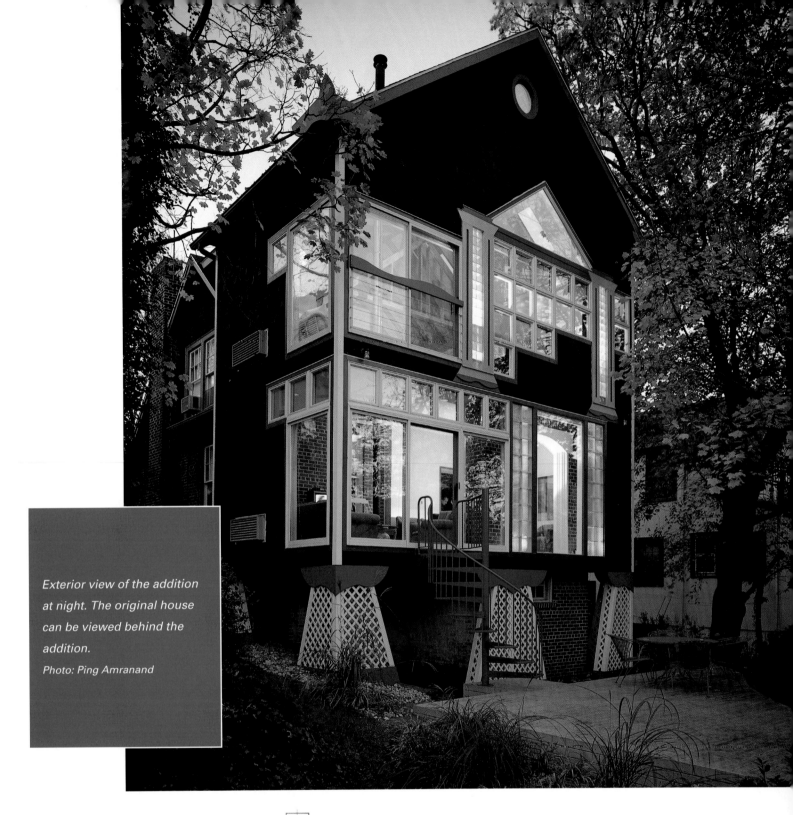

Exterior view of the addition at night. The original house can be viewed behind the addition.

Photo: Ping Amranand

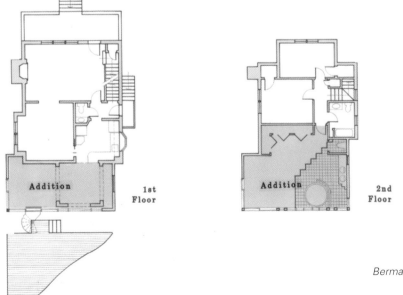

Addition   **1st Floor**

Addition   **2nd Floor**

OSEH SHALOM SYNAGOGUE

Laurel, Maryland

The Oseh Shalom Synagogue is located at the intersection of two suburban roads in Laurel, Maryland. The building is designed to sit on the corner and create an urban scale rather than an exposed parking lot. The building design responds to the site with two distinct expressions.

The highway side is monumental and dynamic. Seen at high speeds, the building's streamlined symmetry emphasizes the domed sanctuary as a focal point. Yet there are touches of asymmetry, such as the large crack in the outer sanctuary wall, which keeps its highway image exciting. This cracked wailing wall represents the notion of incompletion until the coming of world peace in the messianic age. The seven stripes of colored Jerusalem stone with winged sky-blue parapets lifting to the heavens are a modernization of Judaic roots from the Holy Land.

Once on the site, the human-scale qualities of the building prevail. Symmetry and uplift are expressed by the clear procession to the dome of the sanctuary. The diversity and complexity of a pedestrian village are expressed by the variety of materials and forms. Sprinkled around the building and in its courtyards are living trees of life, which reinforce a constant intermingling of nature and building.

The building plan uses symmetry and corridors surrounding courtyards as the main circulation area as well as the natural concentric center of day-to-day activities. Natural light is introduced into every room with glazed courtyards and doors, the translucent dome, windows, and skylights. The building is passive-solar heated and is super insulated for low energy consumption. Cross ventilation through the courtyards and operable windows allow for significant energy savings in this moderate climate.

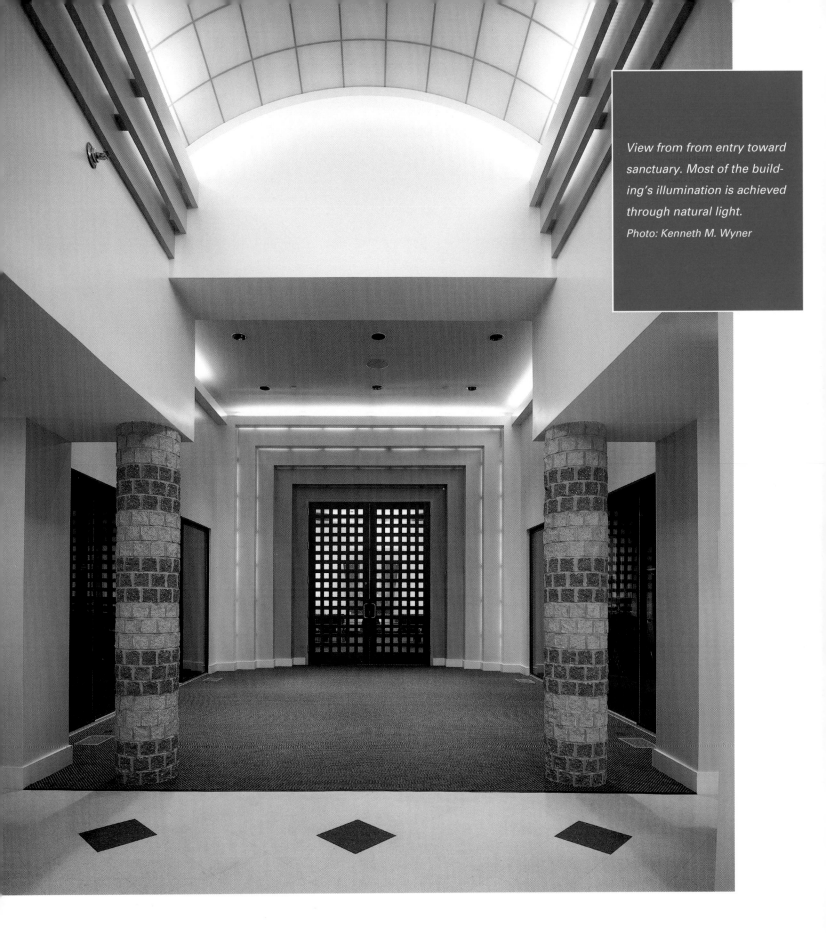

View from from entry toward sanctuary. Most of the building's illumination is achieved through natural light.
Photo: Kenneth M. Wyner

CARLETON RESIDENCE

This 7,000-square-foot house was designed for a site abutting Washington's Rock Creek Park. The southerly view is a beautiful expanse of the park.

The client wanted a mixture of Japanese serenity and Swedish simplicity as an overall design theme. The exterior's cascading volumes inspired by the Potala in Tibet were designed to integrate with the natural hillside, resulting in a passive solar view of the park. The house is super-insulated and the lap pool serves as a solar heat sink. Along with the conventional kitchen, bath, and bedroom program is a rooftop meditation tower with views of the mountainous copper roof pyramids overlooking the park.

Buddhist tranquillity permeates the property. Walking up the entry path to a 14-foot-high Torii gate, one's reflection can be seen in a black glass wall through green stalks of bamboo. In this entry garden of glass block is another hidden path, and, as a door opens, one is swept up by the granite contours to a fire centered in a black granite cube.

The garden paths around and through the house form a continuous series of processions that celebrate the never-ending quality of nature. An extensive owner-nurtured bonsai collection creates a meditative landscape both inside and outside the house. The exterior is a harmonic collision of acrylic stucco, copper, glass block, PVC pipe, steel, and porcelain enamel.

TOP: *Lap pool and bonsai. This space serves as a solar heat sink.*
Photo: Kenneth M. Wyner

LEFT: *A curved metal railing surrounds the interior stairs. These forms echo the shapes of organic growth.*
Photo: Kenneth M. Wyner

A view into living room from the south side of the house. This side of the house also affords views of a large public park.
Photo: Kenneth M. Wyner

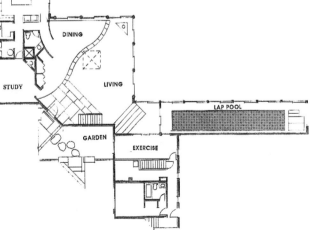

DAVENPORT RESIDENCE

McLean, Virginia

This house is a cubist expression, the overall intention of which was to segregate the design into three distinct forms: the fulcrum tower of bedrooms, the sweeping highway of living room and kitchen, and the tilted solar shaft housing the lap pool. Subtle color variations on the house's synthetic stucco skin highlight the form.

The Davenport house dramatizes a number of energy-conscious design techniques used in response to the diverse climate of northern Virginia. A super-insulated frame reduces overall energy demands, while the southern glazing and large overhangs contribute to passive solar heating and shaded cooling of the interior. The pool is a natural heat sink in the winter, and is separated from the main house in summer by interior sliding glass doors. The operable skylights and roof-vented fan cool the pool area in the summer.

The main house has a rooftop summer fan for venting the whole house at night. All of the glazing opens for cross-ventilation. The operable small square windows above the ground-floor sliders cool the house at night without a loss of security. Low voltage lighting complements abundant natural light. Finally, a wood-burning stove gives the home a heat boost in the winter.

TOP: *Dining room bay window. This element serves as a link between the first floor and the second story.*
Photo: Bruce Katz

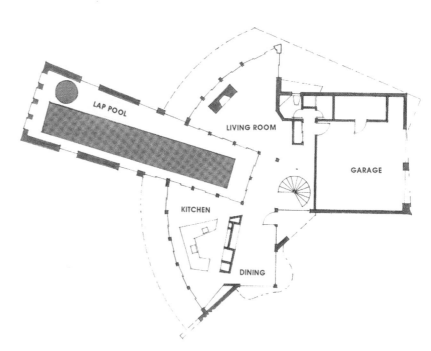

LEFT: *Three-story spiral stair. In the plan, this element acts as a fulcrum, on axis with the lap pool.*

BOTTOM: *Dining room shading overhang. A scupper element removes water from the roof.*

View of the south elevation at night. The slanted window wall is found in the lap pool wing, which serves as a heat sink.

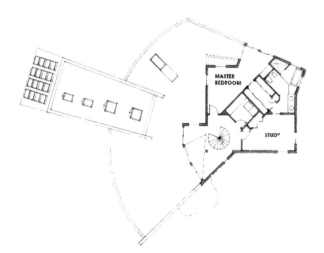

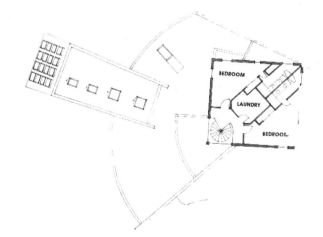

RIGHT: *Dining room offers views toward canted wall. Interior light colors bounce natural illumination.*
Photo: Bruce Katz

BOTTOM: *The kitchen has an open, light atmosphere, with a wall of windows.*
Photo: Bruce Katz

DOUGHERTY + DOUGHERTY

Environmental design is the fundamental basis for our work. We continually balance those interdisciplinary aspects of architectural practice that have drawn us to the profession: creativity, technology, planning, social responsibility, sociology, and a commitment to shaping the future. Environmentally responsive design is an integral part of each of these disciplines.

Creativity manifests itself in human expression. It is the challenge to redefine the known in new ways. It is imagination and visualization. Creativity is the conscious decision to push our thoughts beyond their perceived borders. The creativity to conserve and respond to our natural resources is our current challenge.

Technology is more than the structural, electronic, and utility aspects of building design. It is also the expanded consideration of low-tech methods for responding to the natural environment. Basic physics taught us about air movement, reflective light and the properties of materials. These most basic and precious features have simply been waiting for us to rediscover them.

Planning helps us to meet our responsibilities and ensure the successful future evolution of our communities. We need to consider cause and effect, adjacencies, culture, and economics to view each project beyond the borders of its designated property line. Any planning effort should consider site, orientation, and climatic features to be successful.

Social responsibility governs the direction of our work. An inherent part of this philosophy is the conservation of material resources and the preservation of a healthy and happy quality of life for everyone.

Sociology demonstrates that the way in which people interrelate and respond to each other is affected by the quality of their environment. The distinction between built and natural habitats becomes blurred in a society's total experience. Architecture has the power to influence social behavior and interaction.

A commitment to shaping our future well-being is the primary reason I entered the field of architecture. As a multidisciplinary integration of art, technology, and human factors the creation of our built environment conjures up images of beauty, responsiveness, safety, and our "preferred future."

My interest is in the design of public facilities that will mold the future. Progressive educational environments, inventive early child development centers, and facilities for higher learning and research capture my interest and passion. To practice architecture in its highest sense is to determine and ensure the future of our society and of the human race as we know it.

— *Betsey Olenick Dougherty*

CENTER FOR REGENERATIVE STUDIES

TOP: *Small seminar rooms benefit from natural ventilation through convection, natural light, energy-efficient artificial light, and low-tech means of air movement. The fan not only cools in the summer, but circulates hot air in the winter.*
Photo: Milroy & McAleer

The Center for Regenerative Studies is a unique research, teaching, living, and working facility providing a new environmental focus and academic program for the University. Passive solar buildings, solar hot water, solar voltaic and wind energy systems, reclaimed water systems, aquaculture, and environmental agriculture programs provide a framework for research and experimentation.

Extensive research into the selection of building materials and products has included considerations of toxicity in production and use, recycled and/or recyclable components, the impact on nonrenewable resources, support of renewable industries, and capabilities of long-term low maintenance and sustained life. Natural products of cedar, Douglas fir, and copper roofing have been carefully chosen as appropriate and enduring building materials, exemplifying sustainable concepts while providing a sensitive and nurturing environment for human interaction and creative thinking.

Rooftop solar panels supply 100 percent of the power to large domestic hot water storage tanks. Electrical use is limited to artificial lighting (energy-efficient HID and PL fixtures), compact electrical space heaters, washing machines (clothes will be air dried), kitchen equipment, and limited forced-air systems. All electrical fixtures have been selected for energy efficiency and sensitivity to manufactured materials.

Full-height glazing with low awning windows face south at public rooms. High transfer grilles and open space provide an air path of travel to higher operable clerestory windows. These windows provide indirect natural light and natural ventilation through convection. Electric ceiling fans are in each room. Outdoor trellises will be covered by rooftop plants for shade during the spring and summer.

LEFT: *Trellises to carry rooftop and ground plane plant materials frame a view looking northwest toward the sunspace building (faculty housing).*
Photo: Milroy & McAleer

BOTTOM LEFT: *Agricultural components of the early master plan.*

BOTTOM RIGHT: *An overall view across the ramp toward the riverfront building (student housing), looking southwest from the rooftop of the seminar building.*
Photo: Milroy & McAleer

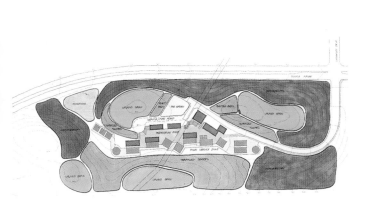

USE ZONE DIAGRAM

N

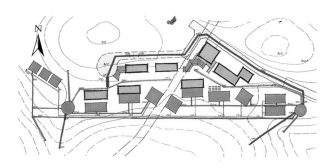

TOP: *Monitors on the seminar building scoop light and air through teaching spaces.*
Photo: Milroy & McAleer

ABOVE: *Water loop concept as it relates to the early master plan. The eventual goal for recycling and reuse remains the same.*

RIGHT: *The riverfront building at dusk, showing its shading features with low sun angles. Shadows also give the building a patterned surface.*
Photo: Milroy & McAleer

OPPOSITE TOP: *The riverfront building is naturally cooled by prevailing breezes passing over the aquaculture ponds and under the building.*
Photo: Milroy & McAleer

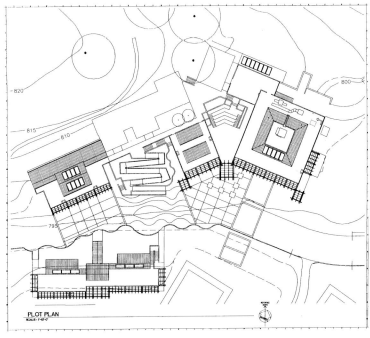

PLOT PLAN
SCALE : 1"=40'-0"

LINE AND SPACE

Photo: Henry Tom

Design must respond to its place. Romantic idealizations of past times and their associative imagery distract one from fitting a site well, responding to climate, utilizing appropriate materials, and meeting clients needs. False fronts are simply false.

Buildings should sit upon a foundation of requirements melded to the site. Magical qualities that make the land special are not to be missed; hydrology, geology, and topography offer design guidance. In the desert the endless horizon, a nearby peak, an Ironwood tree, or a giant Saguaro all inspire and move the hand. The sun tugs at roof lines pulling them way beyond the wall.

Movement from the extreme brilliance of sunlight to the electric bulb and the often large differential between indoor and outdoor temperature has led us to search for ways to avoid abruptness. We attempt to make sequences that allow the body to adjust to change by blurring the distinction between inside and outside. Often we pierce overhangs, so necessary to provide shade, to create a zone that is neither dark nor bright. Our bodies adjust.

By extending the usability of outdoor space we can save tremendous amounts of energy. Functions that would normally be indoors may take place in tempered microclimates. Deciduous plants offer shade in the summer while inviting winter sun to penetrate. A covered, but not interior, area may be made substantially more comfortable by adding a minimal amount of cooling; exhaust air may be directed for a more welcome use.

Water is precious. Lowflow devices and recycling are imperative. The waste water from washing, drinking, and mechanical equipment can feed a gray-water toilet flushing system or irrigation. A desert fountain filled in a downpour can celebrate that giver of life as it empties endlessly in a slow but melodic drip awaiting the next cloud burst.

Natural materials play an important role in the organic relationship that welds structure to earth. Stone, gathered from the site during excavation, quarried at the surface, or salvaged, is durable, beautiful, and may be utilized at little additional cost to the environment. Appreciating the qualities of simple materials leads us to greater sustainability. For example, concrete floors often considered only a substrate may be finely finished, not requiring additional layers ofmanufactured products to hide them. As messengers of environmental awareness we step lightly on the land, creating buildings that invite without shouting. Green architecture is not the latest fad but responsible design.

— *Les Wallach*

Photo: Bob Freund

ARIZONA STATE DESERT MUSEUM

Tucson, Arizona

This desert museum employs architecture that relies on environmental response as its primary determinant. Designed to seat 350 persons in two restaurants served from a single kitchen, this facility explores the use of creating tempered microclimates, water reuse, and salvaged materials. The form of the building was derived by providing shade, responding to vegetation, and fitting the terrain while framing magnificent views.

Visitors enter after a desert experience that leads them to a 180-foot-long ribbed spine. The spine is a shaded transition in the summer and playful shadow projections taking advantage of low winter sun angles.

Outside spaces are cooled to extend their useability. In one instance, exhaust air is delivered to a plenum with twenty-four spot diffusers, each separately adjustable, allowing individuals to modify the climate of their immediate surroundings.

Many of the building walls are faced with stone salvaged from excavation for a nearby elementary school. This material, requiring no manufacturing, adds a timeless beauty that blends the building to the site. Gray water is captured and recirculated to flush toilets. Rain is captured for irrigation and as a source for fountains.

The finishes of the restaurant
complex reflect some of
the cultural images of the
Southwest: native stone, wall
planes, and strong color.
Photo: Henry Tom

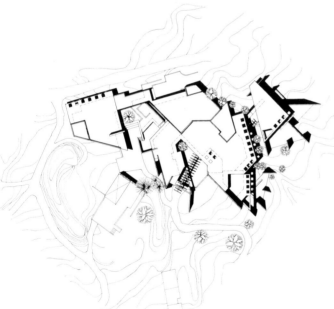

TOP: *A brightly colored shade structure serves as a way-finding device to draw patrons in from the exterior paths.*
Photo: Henry Tom

BOTTOM: *The restaurant complex's mendering plan forms dining areas and outdoor terraces that place the visitor at the desert's edge.*
Photo: Henry Tom

TOP: *The building footprint was manipulated to miss locations of significant vegetation and stop with existing sloping terrain.*
Photo: Henry Tom

LEFT: *The streamlined guardrails provide a gentle visual transition from terraces to distant desert views.*
Photo: Henry Tom

BOTTOM: *Angled walls faced with native stone proved a gradual transition at the desert's edge.*
Photo: Henry Tom

BOYCE THOMPSON ARBORETUM VISITOR CENTER

TOP: *The "slabless" waffle system allows the option of leaving spaces open to the sun, closing the spaces with shades, or installing acrylic domes to assist in botanical research.*
Photo: Henry Tom

W hen Colonel William Boyce Thompson decided in the early 1920s to establish and endow an arboretum, he declared his determination to "build the most beautiful and most useful desert garden of its kind in the world." Over the past sixty years his dream that the arboretum "be for the benefit of all mankind" has become a reality. Set in the rugged land of legend and natural beauty, his arboretum is one of the oldest botanical and research gardens in the American West.

The new visitor center provides an introduction to the arboretum's unusual botanical collections and interpretive programs. Visitors continue directly from the center onto the main trail. Indoor and outdoor spaces were designed to flow naturally one into the other. Concrete and stone walls penetrate the inside of spaces while wood ceiling material and brick flooring crosses the exterior space to join interior functions visually.

This project responds to its desert site. It demonstrates the use of both visual and thermal transitions. One enters either from parking lot or the trail into a partially shaded area under the grid. As the eyes and the body adjust, the visitor moves into fully shaded, then externally cooled, space prior to entering air-conditioned interiors. An outside display area is evaporatively cooled from below by a thirty-foot-high evaporative cooler that is expressed at the entry.

A concrete roof grid unifies the project while offering flexible environmental control by allowing scientists to "plug in" skylights of varying transmissivities or shade devices as appropriate for differing plant requirements. Water recaptured from roof structures, lavatories, and floor slab water runoff (both rain and irrigation) is stored for recycling.

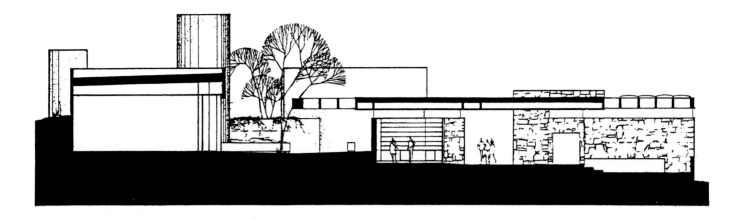

The funnel-shaped walls of the entry help cool by capturing the wind and accelerating it as it narrows into the actual opening of the building.
Photo: Bob Freund

LEFT: *Interior view looking toward covered plant sales area.*
Photo: Henry Tom

BOTTOM: *By creating partially shaded areas, then fully shaded exterior areas prior to entry of interior spaces, the eyes and body acclimate.*
Photo: Bob Freund

OPPOSITE TOP: *Straddling the main entry trail, the structure is designed to house interpretive, administration, and retail functions while demonstrating appropriate desert architecture.*
Photo: Bob Freund

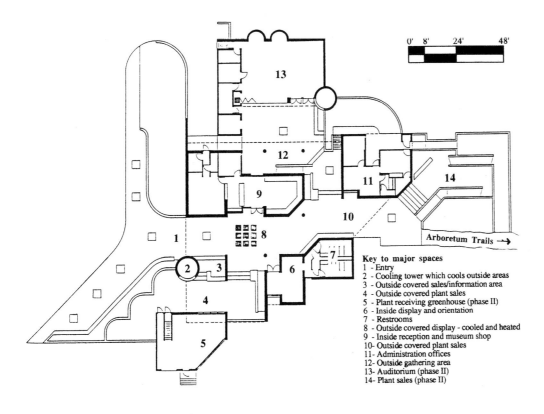

Key to major spaces

1 - Entry
2 - Cooling tower which cools outside areas
3 - Outside covered sales/information area
4 - Outside covered plant sales
5 - Plant receiving greenhouse (phase II)
6 - Inside display and orientation
7 - Restrooms
8 - Outside covered display - cooled and heated
9 - Inside reception and museum shop
10- Outside covered plant sales
11- Administration offices
12- Outside gathering area
13- Auditorium (phase II)
14- Plant sales (phase II)

TOP: *South facade showing how building fits into site. Stone walls and blue standpipes and fascias blend into both the terrain and sky.*
Photo: Bob Freund

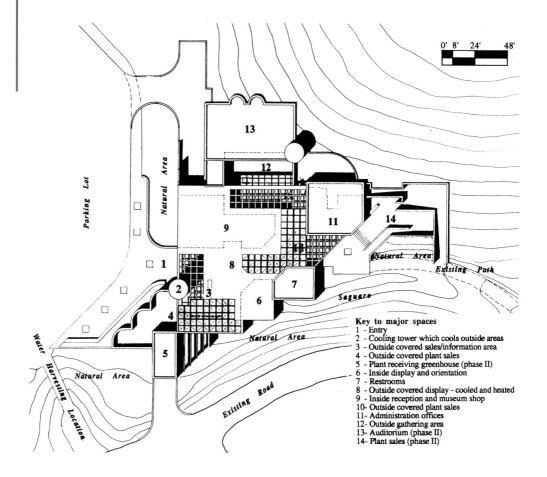

Key to major spaces
1 - Entry
2 - Cooling tower which cools outside areas
3 - Outside covered sales/information area
4 - Outside covered plant sales
5 - Plant receiving greenhouse (phase II)
6 - Inside display and orientation
7 - Restrooms
8 - Outside covered display - cooled and heated
9 - Inside reception and museum shop
10- Outside covered plant sales
11- Administration offices
12- Outside gathering area
13- Auditorium (phase II)
14- Plant sales (phase II)

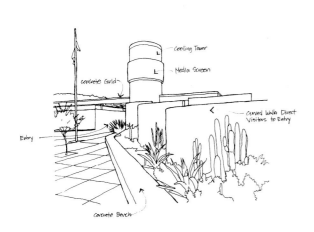

TOP: *View of the cooling tower at the entry. This element helps cool the outside display area.*
Photo: Bob Freund

LEFT: *Standpipe carries recaptured water from the roof away to the central storage system for later uses, such as plant watering.*
Photo: Henry Tom

PROJECT POTTY

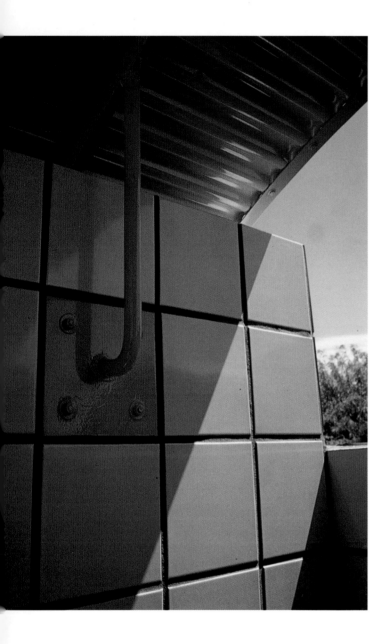

Along the banks of the Canada del Oro, Pantano, Tanque Verde, Santa Cruz, and Rillito Rivers in Pima County, Arizona stretch sixteen miles of linear parks. This is only the first phase of a project that will one day encompass some 105 miles along Tucson's largest washes, and provide the local residents with a neighborhood recreation greenbelt — an oasis along the riverbeds.

The design of the park restrooms involved an evaluation of what a public restroom actually might be. As a prototype, they were conceived as facilities that would break certain stereotypical patterns in public restrooms. For example, environmental factors were fundamental when looking at the restrooms' functional requirements. Natural ventilation is provided by wind-driven turbines that eliminate the need for electrical equipment. An exterior hand sink placed in a garden setting rids the facility of the smells and dirt that usually accompany indoor public lavatories. The gray water from this sink is fed to nearby plants and trees.

The solution was both sculptural (lending beauty to the parkscape) and modular (providing a generic "kit of parts" that could be modified to make the facilities site-specific). The design was based upon actual needs rather than preconceived notions, and among these determinants were issues of function, handicapped accessibility, maintenance, contextual and site issues, territoriality, way finding, visual aesthetics, and cultural response.

This project is a contribution toward creating places that have the potential to enhance both the natural and social environments of our cities.

The simple, geometric shapes, indigenous materials, and bright colors are well received by nearby residents. Photo: Bob Freund

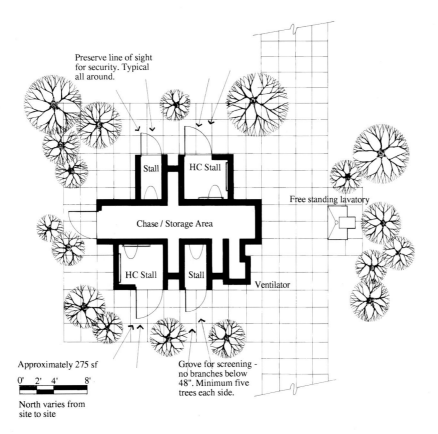

Preserve line of sight for security. Typical all around.

Stall

HC Stall

Chase / Storage Area

Free standing lavatory

HC Stall

Stall

Ventilator

Approximately 275 sf

0' 2' 4'   8'

North varies from site to site

Grove for screening - no branches below 48". Minimum five trees each side.

LEFT: *A brightly colored tower ventilates the restrooms without the use of electrical equipment; a three-mile-per-hour wind is sufficient to exhaust the spaces.*
Photo: Henry Tom

BOTTOM: *The design of these facilities is based upon modules that capitalize the economies of repetitive design while allowing for modifications to make the restrooms unique to each river system.*
Photo: Henry Tom

OPPOSITE TOP: *The restrooms were an opportunity to realize such facilities as sculptural objects.*
Photo: Bob Freund

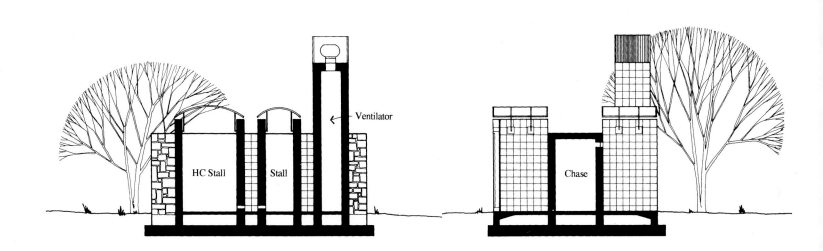

HC Stall   Stall   Ventilator

Chase

SITE ARCHITECTS, ARTISTS & DESIGNERS

New York, New York

As a preface to commenting on the recent work of SITE, I feel I should mention the range of interpretations the word "green" now has in architecture. In point, the term is in danger of becoming as overexposed and irrelevant as tags like "postmodernist" and "deconstructivist" were a few years ago. For those long associated with environmental issues, the recent surge of media hype (and its frequent misunderstanding of real issues) has provoked a need to distance oneself from anything in cocktail conversation and the press that smacks of "green." Still, the label seems universal and here to stay; so, it is worth noting the various interpretations and ideological camps that prevail.

Green architecture can refer to the lingering 1960s advocacy of minimal-tech–geodesic domes, mud-brick houses, solar dwellings, and isolated communes, that rejects any association with the dreaded industrial/military insanity. There are the ecoglobal unifiers who propose that habitat should be linked, like ecology itself, to an infinitely complex, worldwide functional system designed to create a universal community of shared resources. Then there is the garden crowd where "green" means trees and a conviction that salvation of humanity is based on less building and more planting.

The term "green" can also refer to the "deep" ecologists who believe that all industrialized living should be curbed in favor of a retreat to Aboriginal-like resourcefulness in nature or, that failing, a return of the earth to the earthworm. In addition, there is the cutting edge of environmental technologists where their buildings are catalog checklists of the latest innovations in low-energy heating, cooling, and construction techniques. Obviously, all of these groups frequently share each other's territories; at the same time, however, there is a kind of competitive "clubiness" and factionalism that persists in the green movement.

In this somewhat embattled arena, SITE's work could probably be categorized as the "art wing" of ecosensibility in architecture. It is our conviction that an awareness of ecology is as much a social and esthetic concept as it is an acknowledgment of nature's integrate processes. We believe, quite simply, that when environmental technology is used in a structure it should be expressed through clear visual means in the final design and that all architecture today should connect in some creative way to its larger context — meaning social, psychological, topographical, botanical, and historical influences.

Virtually all of SITE's buildings and public spaces reflect the philosophy that environmentally conscious architecture should demonstrate this connection through esthetic choices and combined visual and technical innovations. This view is supported historically by those glorious climate-conscious cities of the Middle East and India where structures sustained their beauty and relevance over the centuries by converting contextual sensitivity into high art. Our influences have been these past examples and we feel our challenge now is to continue to seek ways to bring buildings and spaces into a similar integration with the environment. For SITE, green architecture is an art, as well as a survival, imperative.

— *James Wines*

BEST FOREST BUILDING

Richmond, Virginia

This building was constructed in a densely wooded suburban area, and sited so as not to destroy existing vegetation. The surrounding forest site invades the structure in such a way that architecture appears consumed by some portentous role reversal — or "nature's revenge." This sense of intrusion by trees and plants is achieved by a massive incision, splitting apart the walls and allowing the heavily forested context to take over. This phenomenon is hyperbolized by the surrounding asphalt, giving the appearance of architecture invaded and consumed by nature. The showroom is cut into a hillside and, in order to celebrate this connection between surface vegetation and geology below, the front facade is constructed to hold back a volume of earth behind a glass wall terrarium.

A 35-foot gap between the facade and the actual front wall of the store and an irregular cleft at either end of the building imply that BEST's regulation brick box has been rent asunder by giant oak trees. Customers make the connection on foot by passing through the glass storefront of the outer facade and crossing a bridge to enter the showroom.

OPPOSITE: *The first edition of the Terrarium Wall. This facade was designed to hold back a volume of earth behind a glass plane.*

TOP: *Corner view of the cut-away facade. This cleft implies that the building has been invaded by giant oak trees.*

LEFT: *General view of segmented structure and invading forest. The architecture appears to have been consumed by the surrounding vegetation.*

ROSS'S LANDING PLAZA AND PARK

TOP: *The entrance arches have a split paving area.*

This riverfront revitalization project is associated with a $100 million mixed-use development project on the Tennessee River. Ross's Landing is an important historic location in the Chattanooga community, as well as the site of the Tennessee Aquarium, the world's only aquarium dedicated to freshwater aquatic life, designed by Cambridge Seven Architects. Because of the imposing mass of the building, the surrounding environment is intended to soften the effect of this volume and integrate it into the traditional riverfront context.

Ross's Landing is treated as a microcosm of the entire city and region including its urban grid and flowing landscape. To create a metaphorically readable and visually appealing equivalent for the township, the site is articulated by a series of thirty-five longitudinal ribbons of paving, water, and vegetation. To further emphasize the cityscape/landscape metaphor, these ribbons compose a rich tapestry of color and texture in the form of twenty-foot-wide, straight-line reflections of the urban grid. Gradually, as they approach the Aquarium, they lose their geometric definition and become increasingly organic in profile, finally metamorphosing into lush bluff, water, and landscape environments that surround the Aquarium and extend down to the riverfront boat dock and small performance amphitheater.

These bands march chronologically through the park. Since each band is assigned a period of years, the park becomes a time-line history of the founding and settlement of Chattanooga. Through the use of artifacts — artwork, landscape, and quotations, the city's rich legacy of Indian history, the Civil War, civil rights, the railroad industry, the first Coca-Cola bottling plant, and the Tennessee Valley Authority — the history of the river to current events is represented.

The plaza riverbed play area for children has its own lifted landscapes. Visitors are invited to meander in this flowing stream.

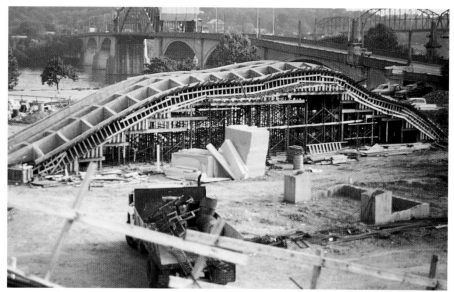

TOP: *View of lifted landscape structure with fountains and waterworks in foreground. This deck leads to the waterfront.*

LEFT: *The lifted landscape, with view toward other ribboned landscape in the distance.*

BOTTOM: *A general overview of the project. The Tennessee Aquarium sits at its center.*
Drawing: James Wines

RIGHT: *Earth-sheltered structure has pedestrian ways beside it. These offer additional access to the waterfront.*

BOTTOM: *The lifted landscape during construction. This man-made landscape echoes the shape of bridges across the Tennessee River.*

AQUATORIUM

TOP: *Rendered perspective of the waterwall and the river that separates the exhibitions from the study center, library, and theater.*

Six months after completing Ross's Landing, SITE was commissioned to develop a concept and design approach for a Phase II environmental center to be situated on Kirkman Hill, adjacent to the landing. The intention is to create a facility that will expand upon the marine science theme of the Aquarium, but not repeat its purpose.

The SITE proposal is for an Aquatorium to serve as an exhibition, research, and recreation building dedicated to the subject of water and people. Its purpose is to explore the earth's most precious resource in terms of science, culture, education, ecology, and health.

The building is designed as a circular structure to conform to the crest of its hillside site, and is composed of a series of narrative walls that separate the functions of the center — exhibits, study, library, theater, health club, and restaurant. Its shape suggests the theme of water and earth, and connects this image to the earliest origins of cosmological symbolism.

The main architectural innovation is the use of lateral walls as the principal sources of information. Rather than treat them as neutral elements that merely support exhibited artifacts, these walls tell the story of water and civilization by means of structural engineering, natural phenomena, and electronic technology. The divisions also create an inside/outside dialogue with the hillsides, using an interplay of gardens, small plazas, and earth-sheltered rooms to increase the fusion of building and landscape. The centerpiece of the main entry hall is a glass-enclosed rain forest garden under a domed skylight atrium. The interior is divided by a massive, undulating, waterwall and river that separates the exhibitions from the study center, library, and theater.

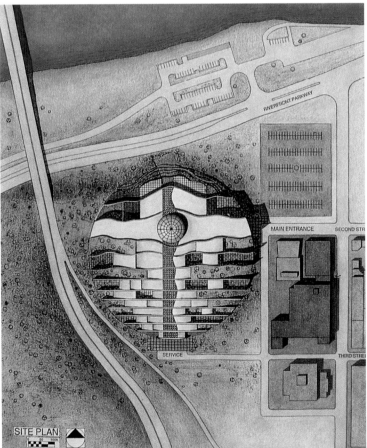

TOP: *Model showing the integration of the building with topography.*

LEFT: *Site Plan. The building's circular form relates not only to the existing topography, but also suggests the theme of earth and water.*

SITE PLAN

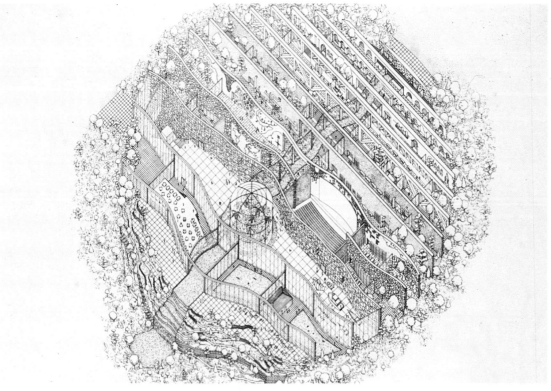

OPPOSITE TOP: *The main entrance, showing the integration of the vegetation.*

OPPOSITE BOTTOM: *Axonometric of interiors spaces.*

RIGHT: *The waterfall and the outdoor recreation area. An interplay of gardens, small plazas, and earth-sheltered rooms fuse the building with the landscape.*

BOTTOM: *The exhibition walls relating to habitat, transportation, and science.*

AVENUE NUMBER FIVE

The undulating waterwall under construction. On the exterior side of this vertical membrane the paving terraces down to suggest the banks of a river and basin.

Avenue Number Five is one of the main pedestrian arteries of the exposition that provides visitors with access to the many national pavilions and displays. The structure is intended to celebrate the topography and history of the Guadalquivir River, as well as to reflect the Expo theme of "discovery," and the technology and environment subtheme.

The concept for Avenue Number Five is to treat the entire length of a grand pedestrian space as a unified experience. This is based on metaphorical references to the Seville River and the need to join a series of disparate facilities — including a monorail station, three restaurants, and two information kiosks — as part of the narrative theme.

In plan, the Avenue is divided to function as a waterwall on one side, and as a grand processional of columns and pergolas on the other. As a simple diagram, the processional is dominated by the straight line of the monorail, which is then intersected longitudinally by an undulating glass waterwall that corresponds to the topography of the river course. On one side of this vertical membrane, the paving is terraced downward in an incremental way to suggest the banks of the river and a basin of water flows from one end to the other. At the west part of the plaza, the source of the river from the mountain is represented by a massive, earth-sheltered structure (an information station), while at the extreme east section a kiosk made entirely of glass sits in a reflection pool, representing the flow of the Guadalquivir to the sea. All of the restaurants are surrounded by the undulating waterwall and each is covered by a roof composed of earth and vegetation, or a vine-covered pergola. These elevated gardens — or "floating landscapes" — provide a unique environmental experience for the arriving monorail trains and offer cooling shade in the waiting areas of the station.

Roof structure composed of earth and vegetation. The structure is comprised of open space-frame trusses and thin wires which serve as an armature for plant life.

TOP AND RIGHT: *Detail of the waterwall. The shape of the waterwall corresponds to the topography of the river course.*

OPPOSITE TOP: *The cafe area under the pergola vegetation.*

OPPOSITE CENTER: *Rendered perspective of the entire project. The concept is to treat the entire length of a grand pedestrian space as a unified experience.*

OPPOSITE BOTTOM: *Columns, which are seeded earth terrariums bound in perforated metal sheathing, and pergolas under construction.*

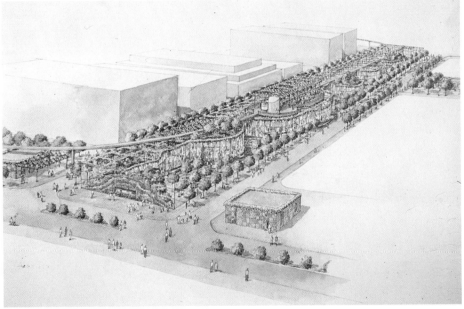

SAUDI ARABIAN PAVILION

Seville World Expo, Seville, Spain

This concept for the Saudi Arabian Pavilion at the Seville World Expo is based on a composite of elements that are characteristic of the Kingdom's architecture and landscape. The building is defined by a rectangular steel grid enclosure reflecting the geometric origin of Saudi arts, crafts, astrology, and Islamic patterns. This also functions as a matrix to support a variety of archaeological and regional design fragments and a group of energy-conservative cooling towers.

The general configuration of the pavilion is based on a generic Saudi structure, with its exterior masonry enclosure surrounding an internal, open air atrium. However, whereas these typical edifices are completely enveloped by dense walls to isolate inhabitants, this Expo pavilion opens up its facade to welcome the world. This has been accomplished by designing the building as a series of overlapping elements in space — with an exterior volume built of mud-brick and stucco — which are cut away to reveal successive layers of structure, vegetation, and architectural artifacts.

The interior courtyard, normally uncovered, is sheltered by a massive tent assembled from hundreds of Bedouin blankets. When viewed from the adjacent monorail train and the pavilion's VIP terraces, this vast collage of woven fabrics and brilliant colors serves as a visual tribute to the regional diversity of Saudi Arabia and its rich crafts legacy.

Night view of the pavilion's facade. The steel grid structure reflects the geometric origin of Saudi arts, crafts, astrology, and islamic patterns.

Detail of the water cooling
system enclosed in glass.
The matrix frame supports a
variety of archaeological and
regional design fragments.

BURT HILL KOSAR RITTELMANN ASSOCIATES

We consider ourselves unique among large architectural and engineering firms in that, beginning in 1972, we pioneered energy and environmental building research well in advance of the current "green architecture" phenomenon.

We design "healthy buildings" that save energy, protect the environment, and promote increased productivity among the building occupants. Healthy building characteristics include indoor air quality, lighting quality, thermal comfort, acoustic comfort, energy efficiency, and environmental responsiveness.

Decisions regarding basic building design and the selection of materials and building systems establish the groundwork for our buildings. Care is also required during construction and commissioning of the building to realize the design intent. Finally, we make sure that those responsible for building operations understand the importance of their actions in maintaining a healthy environment.

After working with our client to establish cost and performance goals for the building, our architects, engineers, and interior designers each identify the building materials and systems that will enable them to meet these goals. Working together, the design team develops an integrated design that will meet the functional and aesthetic requirements, as well as the environmental performance goals.

In the case of indoor air quality, for example, our approach is always to first minimize sources of pollutants, and, second, to mitigate their effects. The team determines how the individual building materials and systems will work together to achieve the best results at the lowest cost. They also develop approaches to construction and commissioning of the building that will help to meet these goals, such as maintaining high outside air ventilation when polluting materials are being installed, and requiring that the mechanical systems be properly cleaned before the building is occupied.

While this example is only one aspect of what we address when designing buildings that are environmentally healthy, it illustrates our approach to all of the elements that make buildings better, more productive environments in which people live and work. Our architects, engineers, and interior designers work together with the building owner to find the best ways to satisfy the special needs of each project.

— _Harry Gordon_

Photo: Maxwell Mackenzie

Washington, D.C.

G reat care was taken to achieve the professionall acoustic quality necessary for studio operations at National Public Radio. Studio spaces were constructed on isolated concrete slabs with sound-rated walls and isolated ceiling systems. All ductwork, piping, and electric conduit penetrations are isolated from both the structure and studio enclosures, as well as isolated from each other. Main HVAC equipment, such as air handlers and pumps, is also independently isolated.

An innovative system of recycling building operations waste was a key part of the renovation. Using an auxiliary elevator shaft, a series of recycling chutes was installed to move material vertically through the building. On each floor, the copy room and kitchen are located next to the recycling chutes, minimizing the horizontal movement of materials.

Building materials were chosen to contribute to the healthy indoor environment. Paints were selected for low emission of volatile organic compounds (VOCs). Carpets and adhesives were also specified to be low-emitting. The gypsum wall board uses "synthetic" gypsum (the by-product of power plant flue gas emissions) and recycled paper. Other interior finish materials and furniture systems were chosen to elimiate formaldehyde and other objectionable chemicals.

TOP: *View from studio 4B into control room. The back panel on the control room wall is used for acoustical diffusion and is made of birch veneer. Flooring is maple, a sustainable source material, of a grade that allows less waste.*

Photo: Maxwell Mackenzie

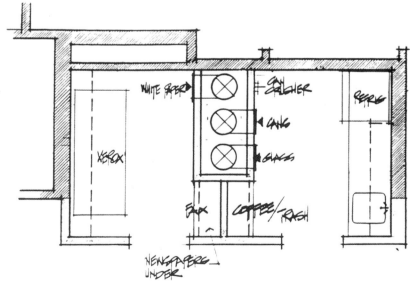

TOP: *View from control room into a recording studio. Walls are made of a synthetic gypsum board covered with recycled paper and painted with low VOC latex paint. Cabinet edging and woodwork is maple.*
Photo: Maxwell Mackenzie

RIGHT: *View from studio 3B into control room. Woodwork is maple, a sustainable source material, of a grade that allow less waste. Furniture is by Herman Miller, a company that uses sustainable materials for its products.*
Photo: Maxwell Mackenzie

DEWEES ISLAND MASTER PLAN

Dewees Island, South Carolina

TOP: *The island sits off the coast of South Carolina. It includes sensitive ecosystems that require careful planning in order to preserve them for future generations to observe and enjoy.*

Dewees Island is located twelve miles off the coast of Charleston, South Carolina. Typical of barrier islands, Dewees has wide stretches of white sand beaches, dunes, salt marshes, and maritime forests.

Burt Hill Kosar Rittelmann Associates was hired to develop a master plan for Dewees that would preserve the natural environment with no negative impact. Thus, an architectural review board has been established on the Island to enforce the low-impact design philosophy. This board must approve design of all houses on the Island, and while no particular style is favored, the Board recommends that designs maintain the regional character of South Carolina's low-country and sea island architecture. These structures are characteristically built on pilings, with wide overhanging eaves and wrap-around porches, operable shutters, dormer windows, steep pitched gable or hip roofs and, frequently, narrow wings. The use of environmentally responsible building materials is encouraged.

The design guidelines strongly recommend careful site planning and orientation of structures to maximize protection from winter winds and summer sun and to make maximum use of natural ventilation and passive solar heating to reduce fuel consumption. In houses, ceiling fans and whole house fans are recommended to reduce the use of energy-intensive air conditioning. Both solar water heating and photovoltaic power are suggested to reduce the use of electricity. Energy-efficient home design is recommended with effective insulation, attic ventilation, and radiant and air-infiltration barriers.

RIGHT: *The island's ecosystems were studied and their preservation incorporated into the Master Plan.*

BELOW: *Infrared photo indicates plant life and complex water ecosystems.*

BOTTOM LEFT: *The design guidelines suggest environmentally sensitive layouts. For example, outdoor living areas should be located to take advantage of the natural site features.*

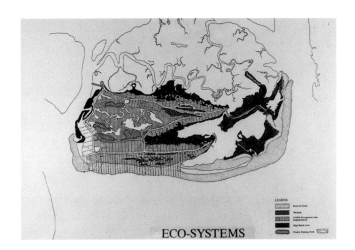

ECO-SYSTEMS

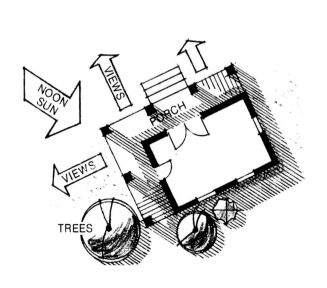

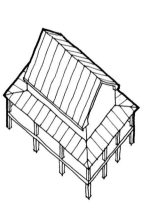

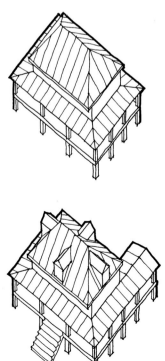

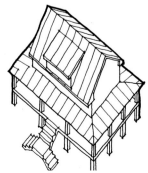

INTERNATIONAL INSTITUTE FOR ENERGY CONSERVATION

TOP: *Energy-efficient lighting is used but not at the expense of a bright office interior. Fixtures are T-8 fluorescents.*

Photo: Victoria Cooper

The mission of IIEC is to foster the implementation of energy efficiency in developing countries, stressing activities that yield real energy savings. Burt Hill's design for the new IIEC headquarters is a demonstration of appropriate technologies and design solutions that contribute to this mission.

The lighting strategies are particularly noteworthy in that they use a combination of techniques to achieve excellent lighting quality with very low energy use within a competitive construction budget. The perimeter offices in the administrative area use daylighting to provide a major portion of the lighting needs, and dimming controls reduce electric lighting levels and energy usage. When the offices are unoccupied, occupancy sensors turn off the lights completely.

In other portions of the offices, direct and indirect lighting fixtures are suspended from the ceiling to provide excellent color characteristics. Manual multilevel switching and dimming controls allow the users to set the lighting level at the best point for different tasks. The lighting quality is achieved with a power budget of approximately 0.8 watts per square foot, putting it among the best of energy efficient lighting designs.

Environmental features are also evident in the office design. The carpet is made from recycled beverage bottles and the tackable wall surfaces in each office are made from recycled paper. Interior windows permit daylight to extend deep into the offices, and allow all users a view of the outside.

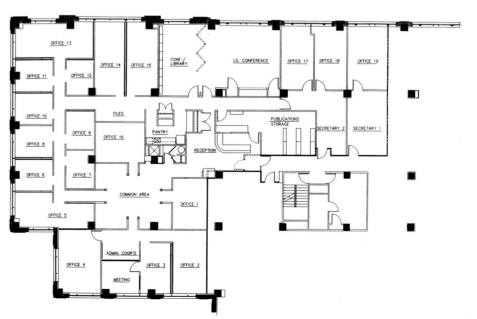

Wall surfaces are tackable and made from recycled paper. Multiple levels for partition heights create a dramatic separation of space, and the brightly colored caps on low partitions establish a color theme that is carried throughout the design.
Photo: Victoria Cooper

SUSAN MAXMAN ARCHITECTS

Philadelphia, Pennsylvania

Photo: Catherine Bogert

Our firm has always practiced "environmentally responsive" architecture by designing buildings that fit into their surroundings, are compatible with the way the users live, and are in harmony with forces operating in the community. In recent years we have focused our efforts even more on what has now become known as sustainable design, or green architecture.

The construction industry continues to have a major environmental impact, generating at least 20 percent of the nation's solid waste, consuming more than 11 percent of U.S. energy, and producing 30 percent of the country's greenhouse gases. As a player in this industry, we believe we are obligated to conduct our business as responsibly as possible. We aim to demonstrate an environmental ethic by adopting sustainable design practices that advocate reduction, reuse, and recycling.

For us, this means transcending the mastery of the construction of a single building by moving on to sharing in the design of whole environments. We do this by practicing an interdisciplinary approach to design and planning. We view our role as a generalist that brings together a team of consultants and leads the total design effort through a consensus-building process. Each member of the project team is made aware of our values and the sustainable design goals for the project. Although budgets and schedules necessarily drive our projects, obtaining a commitment by all members of the project team up front allows us to optimize our consultants' expertise and helps ensure that opportunities are not missed.

We advocate resource efficiency, that is, any aspect of a project that makes better use of resources through both natural and technological strategies than would normally occur with conventional practices. Examples from recent projects include waste reduction techniques, such as the reuse of existing buildings, material salvage, construction site recycling, specifying recycled content building materials, and designing for user or occupant recycling programs. Other examples involved energy conservation measures such as passive solar design, daylight optimization, use of occupancy and light sensors, and fuel source evaluation.

Through continuing education and active research, we have become specialists practicing a design philosophy that emphasizes quality of life, cost effectiveness, and a concern for the future. By evaluating the materials and systems that go into a project's design to conserve natural resources, decrease environmental degradation, and create healthy buildings, we are planning now for the future.

— *Susan A. Maxman*

CAMP TWEEDALE

Oxford, Pennsylvania

This award-winning project for the Freedom Valley Girl Scout Council presented a unique set of requirements: a cluster of winterized buildings, including four sleeping cabins and a dining/activity building, on a site traditionally used only for summer tent camping.

Nestled at the edge of a hilltop clearing to minimize site disturbance while maximizing views to the outdoors and solar orientation, the rustic sleeping cabins create the feeling of tent camping although they are heated and can be used year round. The dining/activity building with its mezzanine, wide steps, and sheltered benches provides gathering places for the campers as they experience the outdoors. The lookout tower, linked to the dining hall by a bridge, serves as a landmark orienting visitors to the campsite.

The four cabins, each with two bathrooms, accommodate twelve girls per cabin in a two-story arrangement. The dining hall features a double-sided stone fireplace, kitchen, and observation tower with views of the adjoining woods, sleeping cabins, and access path. The architects designed all utilities for the site, including a new septic system, new winterized water service lines to an existing well, and new electrical service.

The roof construction for all five buildings makes use of rigid insulation. The structures are cooled passively during temperate months with operable windows and screen doors that facilitate cross ventilation of all spaces. The porch of the activity building shades the dining hall from late afternoon summer sun, while clerestory windows allow hot air to be vented.

Wood was used extensively throughout the buildings for exposed structure, as well as for interior and exterior finishes. It was selected because it is inherently sympathetic to the natural environment of the project's setting, and, when properly specified, represents a renewable resource.

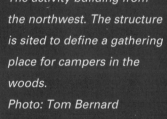

The activity building from the northwest. The structure is sited to define a gathering place for campers in the woods.
Photo: Tom Bernard

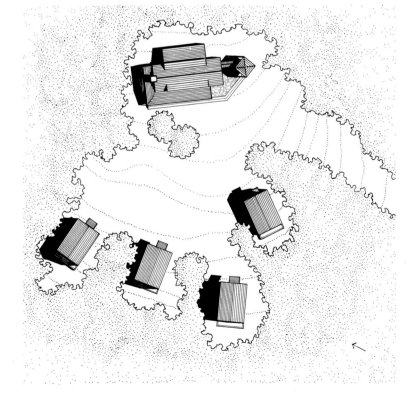

TOP: *Activity building from the south, with its lookout tower. Porches provide shaded respites in the woods.*
Photo: Tom Bernard

LEFT: *Detail of wood structure at activity building. The material was chosen partly because it is renewable.*
Photo: Jeffrey C. Hayes

OPPOSITE TOP: *Detail of dining hall loft. The wood was finished to accent the grain of this natural material.*
Photo: Tom Bernard

OPPOSITE BOTTOM: *Dining hall interior with large fireplace as focus. Note the exposed wood roof structure.*
Photo: Tom Bernard

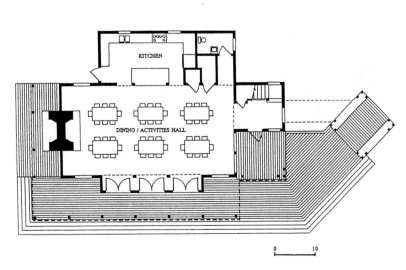

KITCHEN

DINING / ACTIVITIES HALL

0   10

Section

Second Floor

First Floor

0   10

OPPOSITE TOP: *One of the camp's simple cabins. As many trees as possible were left undisturbed.*
Photo: Tom Bernard

OPPOSITE BOTTOM: *Porches with built-in benches provide welcome places to sit.*
Photo: Susan Maxman

RIGHT: *Cabin interiors have a light, expansive atmosphere. Natural light provides an alternative to energy use.*
Photo: Tom Bernard

BOTTOM: *Cabins as they are grouped around a forest clearing. Trees provide some privacy between each cabin.*
Photo: Tom Bernard

WOMEN'S HUMANE SOCIETY ANIMAL SHELTER

Bensalem, Pennsylvania

TOP: *Kennel elevation detail. Exterior is clad in low maintenance corrugated metal siding.*
Photo: Catherine Bogert

This project includes new construction of full service facilities for an animal shelter on an 11-acre suburban site. The 24,500-square-foot program includes an administrative area with offices for management, education, humane and cruelty investigation staff, a conference room, and a multipurpose community room.

The building features a high efficiency mechanical system with variable volume controls in each room. Since refrigerants with chlorofluorocarbons (CFCs) have been linked to the destruction of the ozone layer, a cooling system was specified that contains no CFCs.

Energy-efficient lighting, consisting of linear and compact fluorescent fixtures with high frequency ballasts and T-8 lamps, was used to reduce electrical energy usage and related costs. Both ambient light and occupancy sensors add to the effort to control electrical energy costs. The building is designed so that 40 percent of its lighting needs are supplied through natural daylight. High-performance-heat mirror glazing, coupled with building overhangs, controls sun penetration into the building. The building's energy-efficient design of building systems and equipment is expected to contribute to an estimated $40,000 in energy savings each year.

Materials were selected emphasizing products that are both recycled and nontoxic. Examples include floor tiles fabricated from glass manufacturing by-products, adhesive backed carpeting which can be installed without toxic glues, minimum 50 percent recycled rigid insulation free of CFC agents, rubber floor mats made of recycled tires, benches and bathroom partitions composed of 65 percent recycled plastics, and low-flow water conserving toilets.

Light-filled kennel interior.
Reliance on natural light
reduces the building's
energy demand.
Photo: Catherine Bogert

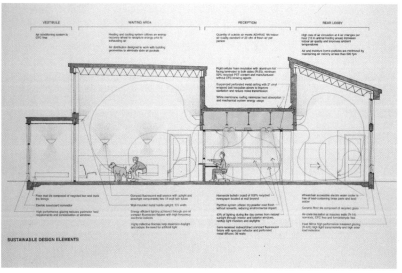

SUSTAINABLE DESIGN ELEMENTS

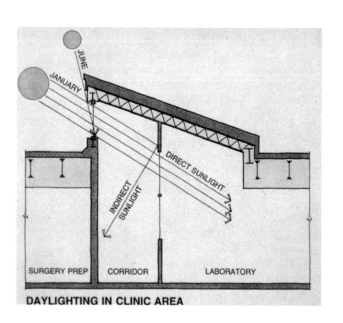

DAYLIGHTING IN CLINIC AREA

OPPOSITE TOP: *Entry to community room. Windows are oriented to naturally light interiors.*
Photo: Catherine Bogert

OPPOSITE BOTTOM LEFT: *Section through lobby indicating sustainable design features.*

OPPOSITE BOTTOM RIGHT: *Daylighting diagram for clinic area. High summer sun is omitted, while low winter sun is gained.*

RIGHT: *View from clinic area looking north. The building's compact form allows more of the site to be used for nature walks.*
Photo: Catherine Bogert

BOTTOM LEFT: *Diagram of energy recovery wheel used in kennels.*

BOTTOM RIGHT: *Section through office indicating sustainable design features.*

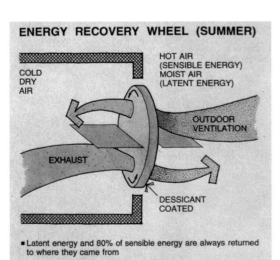

ENERGY RECOVERY WHEEL (SUMMER)

COLD DRY AIR

HOT AIR (SENSIBLE ENERGY)
MOIST AIR (LATENT ENERGY)

OUTDOOR VENTILATION

EXHAUST

DESSICANT COATED

■ Latent energy and 80% of sensible energy are always returned to where they came from

■ Energy Recovery Wheel used only in kennel and clinic areas where there are 8-10 air changes per hour

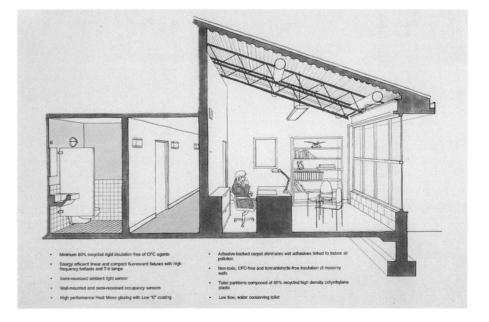

- Minimum 50% recycled rigid insulation free of CFC agents
- Energy efficient linear and compact fluorescent fixtures with high frequency ballasts and T-8 lamps
- Semi-recessed ambient light sensor
- Wall-mounted and semi-recessed occupancy sensors
- High performance Heat Mirror glazing with Low "E" coating

- Adhesive-backed carpet eliminates wet adhesives linked to indoor air pollution
- Non-toxic, CFC-free and formaldehyde-free insulation at masonry walls
- Toilet partitions composed of 65% recycled high density polyethylene plastic
- Low flow, water conserving toilet

TOP: *Detail at rear courtyard. Heat mirror glazing and over-hangs control solar penetration into building.*
Photo: Catherine Bogert

RIGHT: *View from community room looking south. An open courtyard admits welcome southern light.*
Photo: Catherine Bogert

TOP: *Elevation of kennel. Low maintenance materials include concrete block and metal siding.*
Photo: Catherine Bogert

RIGHT: *Corridor in clinic area. High windows allow natural illumination but maintain privacy.*
Photo: Catherine Bogert

ALICE C. TYLER VILLAGE OF CHILDHELP EAST

TOP: *Buildings incorporate natural materials from renewable sources. Natural daylighting is gained through clerestories, light monitors, and skylights.*

Childhelp USA is a nonprofit organization dedicated to the care of abused children. Its new home will be on an 11-acre site with eight new residential cottages for children ages 12 to 16, and a small school complete with gymnasium and cafeteria.

Energy analysis software is being used to capitalize on energy conserving, high performance, passive solar design strategies for the cottages and the school. This involves detailed study of the buildings' orientation; amount of glazing; and typical wall, floor, and ceiling construction, with consideration given to local weather and solar data.

Natural, passive cooling through the use of operable windows will be employed throughout the project, supported by mechanical systems as needed. Since refrigerants with chlorofluorocarbons (CFCs) have been linked to the destruction of the ozone layer, a mechanical cooling system will be specified that contains no CFCs.

Energy efficient light fixtures combined with extensive use of natural daylight through clerestories, light monitors, and skylights will reduce the amount of electrical energy that the village uses. Both ambient light and occupancy sensors strategically placed in rooms will add to the effort to control electrical costs.

Recycled and non-toxic building materials are being investigated with an eye towards not only how they have been manufactured initially, but also their long-term impact after installation. Examples include lightweight reinforced concrete block fabricated from wood and paper by-products, insulation made of 50 percent recycled content, and cedar siding manufactured by a company practicing sustainable yield forestry.

TOP: *Orientation of buildings is determined with the aid of energy-analysis software.*

RIGHT: *Overall view of the village plan. The 11-acre site design will preserve the bulk of the existing vegetation.*

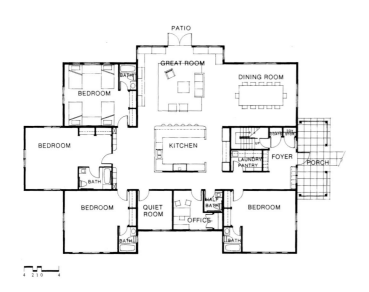

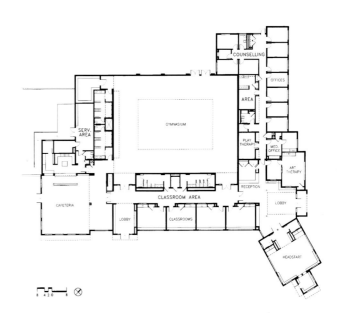

JAMES CUTLER ARCHITECTS

Photo: Pam Cutler

People and their needs are only one part of the complex system of relationships that comprise life on this planet. Our power to damage or destroy these systems mandates the responsibility to exercise careful stewardship of the land.

Thus, we are driven to generate site plans and buildings that fit into the landscape while revealing more fully its nature and beauty. To this end, we have developed methods of design and construction that allow us, our clients, and our contractors to have a higher sensitivity to the uniqueness and particularity of a place.

For example, instead of hiring a surveyor, the principal, the project architect, and, if possible, the owners, personally survey the topography and tree positions. By physically apprenticing ourselves to the land we learn its nuances and secrets in a way that no technical drawing can reveal. We design the sequence of arrival to a building in such a way that has the least physical impact on the land. One's passage through the land is choreographed so that its hidden beauty may be observed and appreciated. We attempt to employ natural, nontoxic materials in the construction and use them in ways that more fully express their nature.

During construction we work with the contractor to limit "incidental" damage to the land by organizing the staging of equipment and materials within defined areas. In addition, access is prohibited into any areas that would not necessarily be disturbed by the building, drives, or walks.

Finally, our goal is to fully integrate the building with the land so that any damage to the land or destruction of its living systems would be seen by the owners as a negative aesthetic and financial impact. It is hoped that this recognition would protect the land from wanton or willful damage by future owners.

— James Cutler

VIRGINIA MERRILL BLOEDEL EDUCATION CENTER

Bainbridge Island, Washington

TOP: *The roof is supported on timber rafters resting on perimeter beams that are strapped to supporting posts and angled braces.*
Photo: Art Grice

RIGHT: *The furniture for the great hall is designed to be sympathetic to the architecture.*
Photo: Chris Eden

At the age of 89, the owner of this estate decided to build an occasional home that would allow him to be near his late wife of 60 years, who lies peacefully at the end of a reflecting pool on this historic family site. The estate is now a semipublic arboretum reserve and, when the time comes for the owner to lie beside his wife again, it will become a small education center and visitors' quarters.

Designed to have a minimum impact on the land, the building is sited in a grove of Douglas fir trees next to a meadow, across which lays the reflecting pool in its own grove of firs. The entry walk, which extends through the building to a viewing deck, is on axis with the gravesite. The building itself is divided into a central living, dining, and kitchen area (future lecture room) and two bedroom suites (future visitors' quarters). The master suite is twisted in plan so that the owner's bed is also in line with the gravesite. The wooden parts of the building are supported on stone piers that reinforce the axis. The stone elements are intended to give a sense of the permanence of the relationship between the owner and his wife.

Because the location of every tree was noted, the building is designed and adjusted so that only two or three trees had to be cut.

Photo: Art Grice

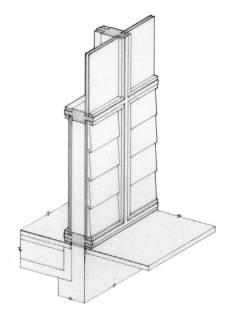

ABOVE: *Detail of the curtain wall.*
Drawing: David Cinnamon

TOP LEFT: *The entrance bridge and the observation walk are on axis with the reflection pool gravesite.*
Photo: Art Grice

LEFT: *Every person involved in the project chose the image of a living thing from the site to be sandblasted into the stone as artificial fossils.*
Photo: Chris Eden

OPPOSITE BOTTOM: *The client's bedroom is slightly off axis to align his bed with the gravesite.*
Drawing: Jim Cutler

Wooden curtain walls are set within the post and beam construction. Note the close proximity of the existing trees to the building.
Photo: Art Grice

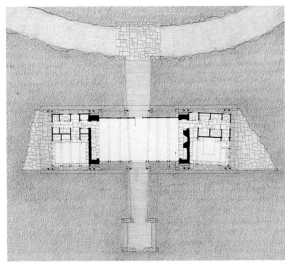

BRIDGE HOUSE

TOP: *Knee braces provide some of the necessary support to span the stream. The length of the span is 42 feet.*
Photo: Art Grice

The site is a heavily wooded, south-facing waterfront lot bisected by a seasonal stream. The stream empties into historic Port Blakely Harbor on the southern end of Bainbridge Island. Permission was granted by the local government to culvert the seasonal stream and fill the streambed to create a level building site.

We convinced the owners of the lot that running the stream through a culvert to develop their land was inappropriate. A developer who shared our convictions toward development of the land was found and worked with us to make this project a model of environmentally thoughtful work.

To minimize the impact on the seasonal stream and existing vegetation, the building is positioned to span 42 feet over the streambed. To minimize environmental pollution, materials such as plywood that contains formaldehyde and other toxins were not used. Instead, traditional techniques such as diagonal shiplap for sheathing and nontoxic stains and paint were employed. The building form relates to the historic mill town character of the existing architecture that lines the harbor.

At the start of construction, all workers were instructed in the value of protecting the site during the normally destructive construction process. As a result of this encouragement, the craftspeople were delighted to be involved in the process and became even more protective of the site than was required.

TOP: *Only one tree was cut down on the building site, and it was used to span the stream.*
Photo: Art Grice

RIGHT: *Site Plan. Note how the building spans the stream.*
Drawing: Jim Cutler

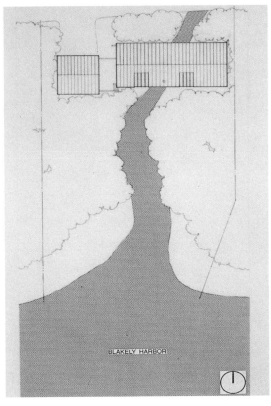

BLAKELY HARBOR

Bridge House 167

TOP: *Windows on the south face are shielded by trees in the summer; in the winter the leaves fall, admitting sunlight.*
Photo: Art Grice

RIGHT: *Second Floor Plan.*
Drawing: Jim Cutler

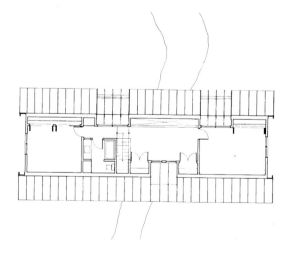

RIGHT: *First Floor Plan.*
Drawing: Jim Cutler

BOTTOM: *Glass hearth tiles allow viewing of the seasonal stream running below.*
Photo: Peter Aaron/Esto

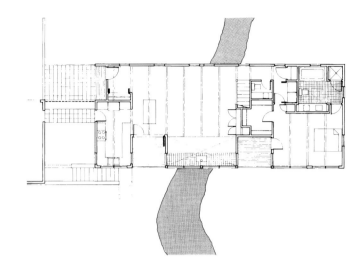

GUEST HOUSE

TOP: *The warm-toned, green-gray concrete contrasts with the meticulously detailed Douglas fir woodwork.*
Photo: Jim Cutler

RIGHT: *Skewing the house away from the concrete retaining wall reinforces the distinction between public and private spaces.*
Drawing: Jim Cutler

The site is located at the southern end of a long meadow allée in a small natural depression. The northern end of the allée is occupied by the owner's existing residence. The whole site is set in a dense fir and hemlock forest with an understory of indigenous evergreen shrubs and ferns.

The owners needed an 1,800-square-foot guest house that would be visually isolated from their existing residence. Besides the internal needs of rooms such as the kitchen and bedrooms, the building would also be able to display a portion of the owner's art collection.

The building was designed to have minimum impact on the land. To maintain visual isolation, the guest house was dug into the existing depression on the periphery of the meadow. The design then became a study of the relationship between a concrete retaining wall and a dwelling. To differentiate the public from the private zones of the building, the wooden structure was skewed to the concrete wall, thus enlarging the entry and constricting the passage from the living room to the bedroom wing. This device also served to further separate the transitory wooden structure from the more timeless concrete wall.

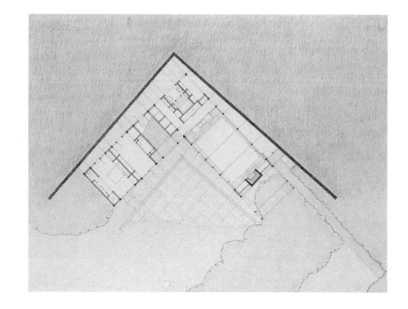

Translucent fiberglass sky-lights the corridor, infusing the house with light, and forming a "light" gasket between the house and the wall.

Photo: Peter Aaron/Esto

LEFT: *While the house is skewed from the wall, the hearth is on axis with it, evoking the contrast between the "found" structure and the wooden tent.*
Photo: Peter Aaron/Esto

BOTTOM: *Windows illuminate the length of the front of the building, and the weathered-colored gray stain helps it appear "tucked in."*
Photo: Peter Aaron/Esto

TOP: The building tells the story of an archaic concrete wall and the organic wood structure that grew out of the remains of that wall.
Photo: Peter Aaron/Esto

RIGHT: The client requested a guest house that would be accessible via a trail through the woods from the main house yet be invisible from the main residence.
Drawing: Jim Cutler

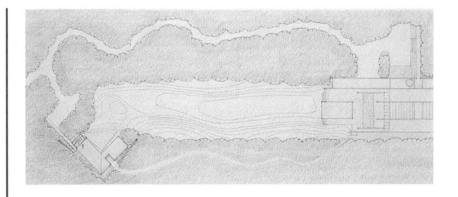

PAULK RESIDENCE

TOP: *Careful siting of each tree on the property allows for this dramatic "floating bridge" entry through the woods.*
Photo: Art Grice

The site is a wooded high bank waterfront parcel on Hood Canal and it faces the Olympic Mountains to the west. The site slopes gently upward to the edge of the bluff before falling off to the beach. The bluff geology required a building setback of 75 feet.

The owners desired a retirement home that focused on the water and mountain views. The residence was to include, in addition to bedrooms, a kitchen, a separate shop, and future detached guest quarters.

The building is designed to maximize the view while keeping any changes to the existing forest to a minimum. It is anchored to grade at one end and, as the grade falls away, the structure remains level, becoming higher and higher above the ground and rising above the edge of the bluff.

During initial design work it was discovered that a walkway perpendicular to the residence could fit between the surrounding trees. This walkway begins at the guest parking and rises up through the understory to meet the residence high above the forest floor. This arrival sequence heightens one's awareness of the forest.

The design of the residence enabled the excavation for the foundation to take place from the inside out, limiting the destruction of surrounding vegetation. The owners hand dug the footings for the walkways to further minimize the removal of vegetation. As construction progressed and areas that were used for staging were vacated, the owners immediately restored those areas with natural plantings.

Standing on the belvedere, which overlooks the Hood Canal and Olympic Mountains, one can turn around and look through the house to the entry bridge on the other side.
Photo: Art Grice

CROXTON COLLABORATIVE

Croxton Collaborative was founded in 1978 and has pursued a multidisciplinary practice consisting of planning, architecture, and interior design. Four basic organizing decisions shaped the early work of our firm: the work should be strongly client centered, context-sensitive, have a unity of planning and urban design with architectural and interior design, and it should be the product of a multidisciplinary team.

Because the client's purposes and the surrounding context were given such weight, many aspects of siting, massing, orientation, and even style were shaped by inherently unique parameters. Therefore, our work is a series of unique identities rather than the sequential evolution of a recognizable design style or expression. Our future work is highly dependent on client referrals and superior project performance rather than marketable visual identity or image.

For these reasons, we were well positioned to take advantage of the opportunities inherent in working with the Natural Resources Defense Council beginning in 1986, and the National Audubon Society in 1989. Out of these projects came a much more fully developed point of view that may best be described as a "value-directed" practice. The same four elements described above serve to summarize this approach.

The most important asset of a client or corporation is the people who work therein. Their health and well being is the central focus around which program, function, and mission are best served. Reestablishing the assets of the natural environment and blending them with the needs and capacities of the built environment can create the highest value, least-impact solutions. Buildings that are increasingly sustainable and ultimately restorative create the greatest value at all levels.

Integrative design, which is inherently multidisciplinary without conventional boundaries, is a precondition of sustainable design. Physicists, geologists, chemists, biologists, energy simulation specialists, and industrial hygienists are among the disciplines to be consulted. Team building should apply not only to the "internal" design team but can be expanded to include all beneficiaries. Utility companies, water districts, storm and sewer districts, municipal solid waste departments, and all other "partners" who benefit from the avoided burdens and costs of minimally compliant buildings can be integrated into the design process through incentive programs, public policy, or direct action by the design team.

Our consensus is that all sound environmental concepts create economies for the built environment as a whole. There is much room for cost-effective and enhanced building, and improved interiors and systems performance. Unfortunately, knowledge to gain these enhancements is not being realized by current project design and delivery methods.

Through a design process that is highly dependent on original research, and based on sustainable, environmental, and human-centered design qualities, we seek to balance the artistic and scientific dimensions of its architecture to achieve the broadest definition of quality and value.

— *Randolph R. Croxton and Kirsten Childs*

NATURAL RESOURCES DEFENSE COUNCIL

TOP: *In office's public spaces, natural light is a distinguishing feature.*
Photo: Marco Ricca

The renovation of the upper three floors of 40 West 20th Street by the Natural Resources Defense Council (NRDC) and Croxton Collaborative stands as a landmark project in the field of sustainable, green architecture.

NRDC, through ground-breaking projects such as the Hood River Conservation Project in partnership with Bonneville Power Administration in Washington State, had already demonstrated dramatic savings potentials over conventional building practice. The key, however, to reaching the majority of owners and builders was to demonstrate a real world "application" accomplished within market constraints. For this reason, NRDC and Croxton Collaborative established the following parameters for the project, in addition to energy, resource and air quality objectives: Available and reliable technology; marketable design quality, workplace amenity, and space standards; market rate construction cost with cost-benefit analysis to support decisions.

During the design process the scope of environmental quality issues was expanded to address building materials impacts prior to their arrival at the site and subsequent impacts in terms of demolition or disposal.

The resulting project established a new standard of energy efficiency for commercial office renovation within a demonstrated cost/benefit analysis, while embodying an environmentally sensitive design that addressed global warming, ozone depletion, toxic materials and gases, and indoor air quality.

Due to enormous public response and media interest, the project has achieved NRDC's goal of demonstrating that high energy efficiency (50 percent reduction) and massively improved air quality (500 percent increase over recommended outside air standard) can be achieved cost effectively. To date, according to Con Edison, no other office building has been able to demonstrate such a low annual energy density for lighting (0.39 watts/square foot with high quality lighting achieved).

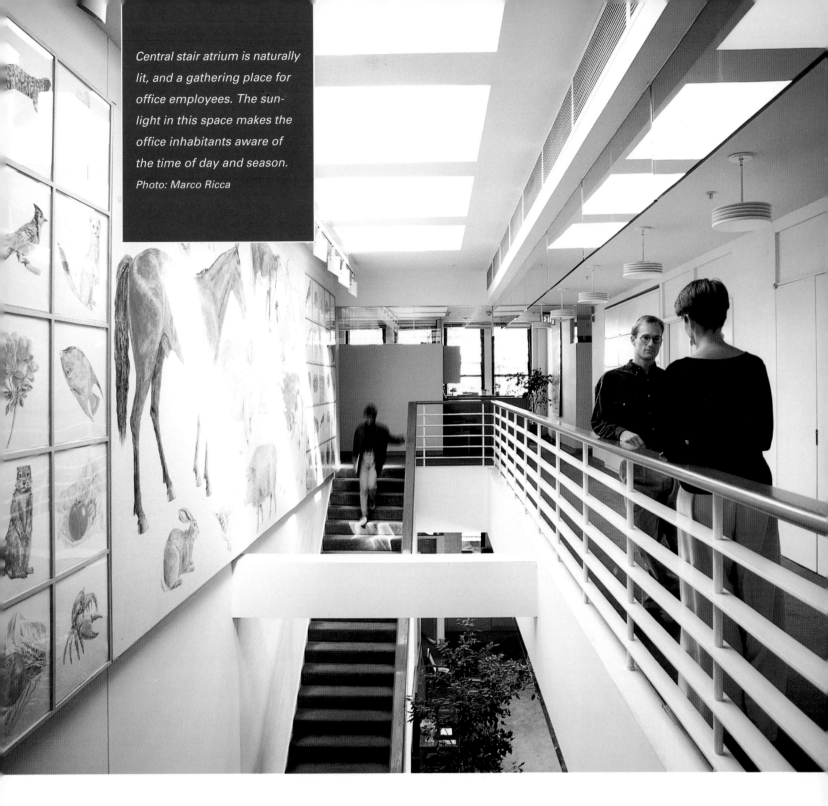

Central stair atrium is naturally lit, and a gathering place for office employees. The sunlight in this space makes the office inhabitants aware of the time of day and season.
Photo: Marco Ricca

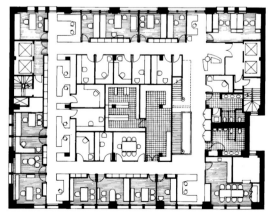

ELEVENTH FLOOR PLAN

0   8   16   32
N

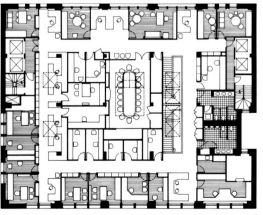

TWELFTH FLOOR PLAN

0   8   16   32
N

OPPOSITE TOP: *Private offices are flooded with natural light. Wood floors were simply refinished, and most of the furniture is recycled.*
Photo: Marco Ricca

OPPOSITE LEFT: *Many of NRDC'S employees commute to work by bicycle; thus, by providing a place to hang a bike, NRDC'S commitment to sustainable technology is further demonstrated.*
Photo: Marco Ricca

OPPOSITE RIGHT: *Private offices are naturally illuminated with windows that cut heat gain. Windows are operable for individual thermal comfort.*
Photo: Marco Ricca

TOP: *White is used throughout the office for high reflectance of light. Natural fiber carpets without off-gassing adhesives were used throughout.*
Photo: Marco Ricca

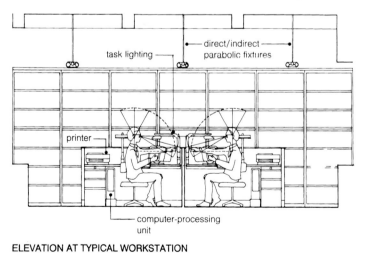

task lighting — direct/indirect — parabolic fixtures

printer

computer-processing unit

ELEVATION AT TYPICAL WORKSTATION

0   3   6   12

New York, New York

TOP: *A historic building in Manhattan was recycled into the new headquarters for the Audubon Society. This approach made use of energy embodied in the century-old structure.*

The National Audubon Society acquired a vacant hundred-year-old commercial structure of historic distinction, the Schemmerhorn building, in early 1990. On the strength of the NRDC project, Croxton Collaborative was retained to undertake the environmentally informed restoration/renovation of the 98,000-square-foot structure for Audubon's new national headquarters.

The inherent advantages of scale, and the ability to design a building-wide mechanical and controls system, allowed not only the enhancement of NRDC strategies, but the expansion of these concepts through new applications.

A dramatic advance came in a five-point program for materials conservation/recycling: recycle the original structure; waste stream separation and recycling of demolition waste; maximum recycled content of new materials introduced; physical plant to support recycling (i.e. chutes, recycle center, composter); and, most importantly, a detailed self-analysis of waste content with coordinated purchase and use program by Audubon (targeting 80 percent).

Nature driven (economizer plate and frame plus 100 percent outside air) and energy driven (gas-fired heater-chiller) was developed to take maximum advantage of outdoor ambient temperature year round. High levels of air filtration (85 percent) were provided.

Most importantly, Audubon demonstrates that if all buildings followed its example in water conservation, solid waste management and support for mass transit, then the next sewer module, incinerator, landfill, or highway project could be avoided. It stands as a challenge to current public policy that fails to reward these great enhancements of existing infrastructure; enhancements which avoid later staggering costs for new infrastructure capacity.

RIGHT: *Stair treads are illuminated with low-wattage lights to supplement natural light throughout the office.*
Photo: Marco Ricca

BOTTOM: *Reception area is naturally lit with a gabled skylight, which is coated to diminish heat gain in the summer.*
Photo: Marco Ricca

LEFT: *Offices take advantage of natural lighting, and share it with interior spaces through the use of glass partition walls.*
Photo: Marco Ricca

BOTTOM: *Furniture throughout the office is made of renewable woods and recycled materials.*
Photo: Marco Ricca

TRANSVERSE SECTION THROUGH TYPICAL FLOOR

TOP: *Electric light levels can be kept low when sunlight is in abundance. Ambient light is supplemented with task lighting.*
Photo: Marco Ricca

RIGHT: *Each floor has recycling chutes for paper, aluminum, plastic, and organic matter, which is sorted in the basement.*
Photo: Marco Ricca

TOP: *The conference room on the roof deck is naturally illuminated, thus cutting energy use. Carpeting without toxic VOCs and off-gassing adhesives was used.*
Photo: Marco Ricca

LEFT: *Penetrations through spaces allow natural light to reach the building's interior. Light colors bounce back light to reach the center of the building.*
Photo: Marco Ricca

VERIFONE COSTA MESA

Costa Mesa, California

TOP: *The rotunda is the central space of the project, with offices clustered all the way around it. It has both UV and infrared filtered light, to give the space color and intensity. All shared public spaces in the project have direct sunlight that marks the time of day.*

Photo: Larry A. Falke

BOTTOM: *Office space adjacent to the rotunda balances natural and artificial light sources. Overhead, bright light comes from a spine clerestory that does not allow distracting direct sunlight into the work stations.*

Photo: Larry A. Falke

VeriFone, an international corporation manufacturing electronic verification equipment, decided in 1991 to initiate a program to upgrade and expand their facilities worldwide in an environmentally informed manner. The first of these, an administrative and distribution center, was completed by Croxton Collaborative and their associated architect Robert Borders in 1993.

At the time, VeriFone occupied a typically featureless, tilt-up concrete building of some 80,000 square feet. This huge, essentially single-story building was located between an airport and a busy highway. The building selected for the first environmental expansion was a "twin" building to the south across a shared parking lot. With only three roadway windows, no views, compromised outside air quality, and a tight budget of approximately $38 per square foot, this project presented a considerable challenge.

The key strategy developed was the maximum utilization and articulation of natural light. In an essentially windowless structure, this was handled in a number of ways, each one appropriate to the activity of the space. Strategies included the use of direct and indirect beam skylights, as well as diffusing skylights coordinated to work with T-8 energy-efficient lighting fixtures in all areas.

A key manufacturing area is 100 percent naturally lit most of the day. Energy-efficient equipment and controls minimize global pollution contributions and the draw-down of Southern California's precious water supply. The HVAC system contains no chlorofluorocarbons (CFCs). The air supply is doubly filtered to provide clean indoor air, and materials are selected to maximize resource conservation and sustainability, and minimize toxicity in the project.

Studies are currently being undertaken comparing this building and its "twin" to determine the improvement in productivity and well being in the renovated building. VeriFone demonstrates that these goals can be achieved not in a future, cost-effective manner but within a current, standard, industrial-building budget.

In the office area, light is received from an overhead clerestory. This space has a view of the light manufacturing area and the loading dock, thus visually linking different functions in the building.
Photo: Larry A. Falke

SUSTAINABLE DESIGN INFORMATION RESOURCES

This list was adapted with permission from the *Sourcebook for Sustainable Design*, available from the Boston Society of Architects.

American Solar Energy Society

2400 Central Avenue, Suite G-l
Boulder, CO 80301
PHONE (303) 443-3130

Publishes *Solar Today*, a national magazine covering solar technologies.

Build Green Hotline

Greater Toronto Home Builder's Association
PHONE (416) 822-4111 x 372

The GTHBA has undertaken a "Build Green Program" to develop public and industry awareness of building materials with recycled content. Their hotline will provide information on a wide variety of such materials available in Canada.

Building With Nature

Carol Venolia
P.O. Box 369
Gualala, CA 95445
PHONE (707) 884-4513

Bimonthly professional networking newsletter on the creation of nontoxic environments.

Center for Maximum Potential Building Systems, Inc.

Pliny Fisk
8604 FM 969
Austin, TX 78724
PHONE (512) 928-4786
FAX (512) 926-4418

Nonprofit education, research, and demonstration organization focusing on the application of appropriate building and resource technology to a range of users, from individual homeowners to regional planning and natural resource agencies.

Center for Resourceful Building Technology

Steve Loken
P.O. Box 3413
Missoula, MT 59806
PHONE (406) 549-7678

CRBT undertakes building projects and disseminates information on resource-wise design, materials, and construction practices. Recently completed a house in Montana using all recycled materials. Offers *Guide to Resource Efficient Building Elements* for $20.

Energy Crafted Home

Northeast Utilities
P.O. Box 2010
West Springfield, MA 01090
PHONE (800) 628-8413

The Energy Crafted Home trains designers and builders in the use of energy-conservative detailing. It is the Northeast Utility Company's program to promote energy efficiency in housing.

Energy Design Update

Ned Nisson
P.O. Box 1709
New York, NY 01938

Monthly newsletter on energy-efficient housing, EDU provides material and product reviews, details, and reports on emerging technologies. $138/year. Cutter Information, the publisher, also publishes *Indoor Air Quality News*.

Energy Federation, Inc.

14 Tech Circle
Natick, MA 01760
PHONE (800) 876-0660
FAX (508) 655-3811

An excellent catalog of energy-efficient mechanical, lighting, water conservation, and weatherization products.

Environmental Building News

Alex Wilson
RR 1, Box 161
Brattleboro, VT 05301
PHONE (802) 257-7300
FAX (802) 257-7304

A bimonthly newsletter on environmentally sustainable design and construction. Product reviews, details, a checklist for sustainable design and construction, feature articles on sustainable building issues. Commercial and residential construction. $60/year.

Environmental Outfitters

P.O. Box 514
New Canaan, CT 06840
PHONE (203) 966-3541

Offers "state-of-the-art" environmentally responsible products for the built environment.

Environmental Resource Guide

American Institute of Architects
1735 New York Avenue, NW
Washington, DC 20006
PHONE (202) 626-7300

The AIA's Committee on the Environment publishes the ERG, an ongoing evaluation of building materials and practices. Eventually, 28 building materials will have been through the life-cycle analysis process. Case studies, reports, and references. $125/year.

Fred Davis Corp.

82 Bridge Street
Medfield, MA 02052
PHONE (608) 359-3610

Catalog of energy-efficient lighting products.

Gap Mountain Permaculture

9 Old County Road
Jaffrey, NH 03452
PHONE (603) 532-6877

The development of sustainable agriculture and culture through homesteads as "living laboratories." Research, workshops, courses, literature on photovoltaics, moldering privies and graywater systems, greenhouses, roof water collection, more.

Home Energy

2124 Kittredge Street, No. 95
Berkeley, CA 94704
PHONE (510) 524-5405

The magazine of residential energy conservation. Works to present a balanced picture of the complex variables affecting energy consumption and conservation. Entertaining and informative. Bimonthly, $45/year.

Housing Resource Center

Al Wasco
1820 W. 48th Street
Cleveland, OH 44102
PHONE (216) 281-4663

Publishes the *Healthy House Catalog*, a primer on residential indoor air quality (IAQ) issues. Also publishes *Your Home*, a monthly newsletter, *Housemending Resources*, a quarterly, and hosts conferences and awards programs on sustainable housing issues.

International Hardwood Products Association, Inc.

P.O. Box 1308
Alexandria, VA 22313
PHONE (703) 836-6696
FAX (703) 836-6370

Industry organization that is beginning to recognize problems and research solutions in current forestry practices.

Memphremagog Heat Exchangers
David Hansen
P.O. Box 490
Newport, VT 05855
PHONE (802) 334-5412

Catalog of energy-efficient mechanical equipment.

NATAS
P.O. Box 2525
Butte, MT 59702
PHONE (800) 428-2525

National Appropriate Technology Assistance Service provides information and technical assistance on renewable energy technologies, including weatherization, energy-efficient building technologies, solar heating and cooling, wind, biomass, alternative fuels, small-scale hydro, PV. Typical users include builders, architects, and engineers.

National Center for Appropriate Technology
P.O. Box 3838
Butte, MT 59702
PHONE (406) 494-4572

NCAT publishes inexpensive booklets on appropriate technology—solar water heaters, composting toilets, biogas, weatherizing a mobile home, more.

NESEA
Michael Grabscheid
23 Ames Street
Greenfield, MA 01301
PHONE (413) 774-6051

The Northeast Sustainable Energy Association (formerly NE Solar Association) advocates for sustainable energy design and construction practices, focusing mainly on residential and light construction.

Nontoxic Environments Inc.
6135 NW Mountain View Drive
Corvallis, OR 97330
PHONE (503) 745-7838
FAX (503) 781-6892

A catalog carrying a variety of nontoxic building materials, including finishes, insulation, joint compound, caulk, ceramic tile materials and adhesives, floor coverings, lighting, water treatment, insecticides, wood preservatives.

Passive Solar Industries Group
1090 Vermont Avenue, NW
Suite 1200
Washington, DC 20005
PHONE (202) 371-0357

Publishers of passive solar strategies.

Real Goods
966 Mazzoni Street
Ukiah, CA 95482
PHONE (800) 762-7325
FAX (707) 468-0301

A great catalog of alternative energy products. PV and wind power equipment, water and air treatment, lighting, electric vehicles, much more. Whole Earth format.

Recycled Products Guide
Mass DEP
One Winter Street, 4th Floor
Boston, MA 02108
PHONE (800) 267-0707

Listing of recycled products available from Massachusetts manufacturers.

Resource Conservation Technology, Inc.
2633 North Calvert Street
Baltimore, MD 21218
PHONE (301) 366-1146

Excellent catalog of energy efficiency building products, details.

The Rocky Mountain Institute
Amory & Hunter Lovins
1739 Snowmass Creek Road
Snowmass, CO 81654
PHONE (303) 927-3851

A nonprofit research and consulting foundation concentrating on sustainability in five areas: energy, water, economic renewal, agriculture, and security. Resource-efficient headquarters/housing built in 1984.

Shelter Supply Inc.
1325 East 79th Street
Minneapolis, MN 55425
PHONE (800) 762-8399

Catalog of resource-efficient building materials.

SERI/TIS
1617 Cole Boulevard
Golden, CO 80401
PHONE (303) 231-7303

Solar Energy Research Institute/Technical Inquiry Service is DOE's technology bank. Disseminates technical documents on energy efficiency and renewable energy, including solar, PV, biofuels, wind energy, ocean energy, energy storage.

Sourcebook for Sustainable Design
Andrew St. John, Editor
Boston Society of Architects
52 Broad Street
Boston, MA 02109-4301
PHONE (617) 951-1433

Invaluable source of information outlets on sustainable design, from which this Appendix was adapted.

U.S. Green Building Council
1615 L Street, NW
Suite 1200
Washington, DC 20036
PHONE (202) 778-0760
FAX (202) 463-0678

A nonprofit consensus coalition of building product manufacturers, environmental groups, building owners and operators, architects, engineers, utilities, state and local governments, and universities. Its mission is to improve the energy and environmental efficiency of the whole building environment.

Yestermorrow Design/Build School
RR 1, P.O. Box 97-5
Warren, VT 05674
PHONE (802) 496-5545

A design/build school that teaches sustainable design to owner-builders and designers.